HUMAN RELATIONS IN SMALL BUSINESS

by Elwood N. Chapman

THE

CRISP

SMALL BUSINESS &
ENTREPRENEURSHIP
SERIES

CREDITS

Editor: Beverly Manber

Layout/Design: ExecuStaff

Cover Design: Kathleen Gadway

Library of Congress 92-54355
ISBN-1-56052-185-6

INTRODUCTION TO THE SERIES

This series of books is intended to inform and assist those of you who are in the beginning stages of starting a new small business venture or who are considering such an undertaking.

It is because you are confident of your abilities that you are taking this step. These books will provide additional information and support along the way.

Not every new business will succeed. The more information you have about budgeting, cash flow management, accounts receivables, marketing and employee management, the better prepared you will be for the inevitable pitfalls.

A unique feature of the Crisp Small Business & Entrepreneurship Series is the personal involvement exercises, which give you many opportunities to immediately apply the concepts presented to your own business.

In each book in the series, these exercises take the form of "Your Turn," a checklist to confirm your understanding of the concept just presented and "Ask Yourself . . .", a series of chapter-ending questions, designed to evaluate your overall understanding or commitment.

In addition, numerous case studies are included, and each book is cross-referenced to others in the series and to other publications.

BOOKS IN THE SERIES

▶ **Operating a Really Small Business**
Betty M. Bivins

▶ **Budgeting: A Primer for Entrepreneurs**
Terry Dickey

▶ **Getting a Business Loan: Your Step-By-Step Guide**
Orlando J. Antonini

▶ **Nobody Gets Rich Working for Somebody Else: An Entrepreneur's Guide**
Roger Fritz

▶ **Marketing Strategies for Small Businesses**
Richard F. Gerson, Ph.D.

▶ **Financial Basics for Small Business Success**
James O. Gill

▶ **Extending Credit and Collecting Cash: A Small Business Guide**
Lynn Harrison

▶ **Avoiding Mistakes in Your New Business**
David Karlson, Ph.D.

▶ **Buying Your First Franchise: The Least You Need to Know**
Rebecca Luhn, Ph.D.

▶ **Buying a Business: Tips for the First-Time Buyer**
Ronald J. McGregor

▶ **Your New Business: A Personal Plan for Success**
Charles L. Martin, Ph.D.

▶ **Managing the Family Business: A Guide for Success**
Marshall W. Northington, Ph.D.

DEDICATION

"Some see private enterprise as a predatory target to be shot, others as a cow to be milked, but few are those who see it as a sturdy horse pulling the wagon."

–Winston Churchill

CONTENTS

INTRODUCTION   iii

PREFACE   xi

CHAPTER ONE   PEOPLE SKILLS ARE CRITICAL   1

Become a People Person 3

It Is Easy to Make Serious People Mistakes 8

Time Management and People Problems 8

The Challenge is Stimulating 9

CHAPTER TWO   IT ALL BEGINS WITH

                                     ATTITUDE   13

You Cannot Play the Game Alone 15

CHAPTER THREE   RECRUITING AND INTERVIEWING   23

Create an Organization Chart 25

Recruiting Applicants 26

Interviewing Applicants 33

Evaluating Applicants 35

Checking References 36

Four Hiring Mistakes You Do Not Want to Make 36

CHAPTER FOUR   ORIENTATION OF THE

                                     NEW EMPLOYEE   39

The Best Human Investment 41

Orientation Goals 41

Seven Steps to a Better Orientation 41

When a New Employee Does Not Work Out 45

CHAPTER FIVE   TRAINING YOUR STAFF   49

The First Thirty Days 51

Seven Steps to More Effective Training 51

Appraising Employee Performance 56

CONTENTS (continued)

CHAPTER SIX   FIVE MAGICAL FOUNDATIONS   59
The Basic Principles 61

CHAPER SEVEN   UNDERSTANDING PRODUCTIVITY   69
The Human Side of Productivity.............................71
Two-Way Communications 73
Psychological Needs 73
Additional Suggestions 76

CHAPTER EIGHT   PEAK AND DOWN PERIODS   79
Staffing and Employee Attitude Considerations 81
Staffing for Peak and Slow Periods 82
Attitude and Inactivity 83
Additional Suggestions 84

**CHAPTER NINE   HOW TO GET HIGHER
PRODUCTIVITY FROM
PART-TIMERS   89**
Lower Personnel Costs and Increase Productivity 91
Ten Tips on How To Achieve High Productivity from
Young Part-Timers 91

**CHAPTER TEN   ACHIEVING THE RIGHT
EMPLOYEE MIX   99**
The Basic Goal 101
Small Business Operations Thrive on Part-Timers 101
Free-Lancers, Consultants and Individuals
Who Work in Their Homes...................................108
Probationary Periods are Essential 110

CHAPTER ELEVEN   COMMON HUMAN MISTAKES   115
Recognize Your Own Weaknesses 117

CONTENTS (continued)

CHAPTER TWELVE   HANDLING HUMAN PROBLEMS   125
The Role of Counseling 127
Rules To Follow 127

CHAPTER THIRTEEN   THE TEAM APPROACH   137
Building a Close-Knit Team 139
Leadership Is the Key 139

**CHAPTER FOURTEEN EXPAND AND EMPOWER
                    YOUR TEAM   147**
After the First Year..149
Sphere of Influence 150
Empowerment Is the Key To Building a Strong
Employee Team 151
Empowerment and Team Collaboration 154

**CHAPTER FIFTEEN   ESTABLISHING YOUR
                    AUTHORITY LINE   157**
The Psychological Environment 159
Mistakes You Do Not Want To Make.........................164

**CHAPTER SIXTEEN   SEVEN HUMAN RELATIONS
                    STRATEGIES   171**
Assess Your Performance 173

**CHAPTER SEVENTEEN SMALL BUSINESS AND
                    THE TELEPHONE   183**
The Heart of Communication....................................185
Telephone Effectiveness Review...............................188

CONTENTS (continued)

CHAPTER EIGHTEEN   **IMAGE BUILDING**   **193**
Selling Yourself 195
Selling Your Image 196
Employees Can Expand Your Trading Area 199
Handling Upset People 200

CHAPTER NINETEEN   **QUESTIONS FROM THE
BACK ROW**   **203**
Train Your Backup Now! 205

CHAPTER TWENTY   **YOUR ROLE AS
A LEADER**   **213**
Do You Have the Right Stuff? 215

ABOUT THE AUTHOR   **227**

PREFACE

Some experts say that if you have enough capital, select the right business, find a 90 percent location, and have a quality product or service that people want, your chances of success are excellent. Right?

Well, almost.

Other experts say that, next to having sufficient capital, the most important ingredient for success is *knowing how to work with people.* The purpose of this book is to present the human dimension of establishing and operating a small business.

At first, it might seem that to accomplish this goal you only need to place yourself in the role of a Human Resources or personnel director. It is much more than that. In a small business, you must build solid, healthy, two-way relationships with employees, and you must do the same with customers, suppliers and professional advisors.

If this book accomplishes its goal, it will convince you that the human side of operating a small business is *as* important as the technical side. It will also help you avoid making unnecessary people mistakes.

Good luck!

CHAPTER
ONE

PEOPLE
SKILLS
ARE CRITICAL

BECOME A PEOPLE PERSON

Whatever your background—technical, manufacturing, medical, academic, farming, management, government, military—you have the right stuff to deal effectively with the human dimension of operating a successful business. It may take a few modifications to your behavior, but you can do it. That is, of course, if you accept the people challenge.

The good news is that you can become a people person by making modest changes and following certain guidelines:

▶ You will not need to make a basic personality change.

▶ You will not need to take clinical courses in psychology.

▶ If you happen to be an introvert, you will not need to become a highly verbal extrovert.

You will, however, need to give the people side of your business the same attention you give to the technical. Maybe more, to:

▶ Develop a new sensitivity to the needs of your employees, customers and resources

▶ Convert your employees into enthusiastic *team* members

▶ Provide learning experiences for employees, quality service to customers, and maintain healthy two-way relationships with professionals you may need to call upon

It is not easy to become a people person, along with financial problems and dealing with everything else—to balance the people dimension with other responsibilities. But, successful entrepreneurs *can* usually do it all. As you quickly discovered when you took the job, when you become your own boss you play many roles.

Harvey became a highly successful engineer for a large firm, but he was never happy and satisfied because of the human conflicts that developed. Some were his fault; others were not. After twenty years, Harvey decided to eliminate the conflicts by opening an engineering service operation. Here, Harvey believed he could build and develop his own staff, maintain relationships with his clients, and eliminate dealing with others who usually did not know what they were talking about.

How did it work out? Excellently, because Harvey assumed responsibility for building good relationships with people in all directions. His comments: "I knew I was capable of building good and rewarding relationships, but with a large company I had to give 95 percent of my attention to engineering problems. People problems were left to others. When I started my own business, I recognized that I needed to take a new attitude toward people, so I changed. My wife claims I am a different person since I have given people equal billing."

When they were approaching their fiftieth birthdays, John and Peg decided to open a picture framing business in a growing community that had already attracted many artists. John left a construction job, and Peg took early retirement from a research laboratory.

How did things turn out? To be truthful, they almost drowned in people problems. After many misunderstandings with customers and suppliers, they sat down with a friend in the same business from a different community to analyze what was going wrong. Their friend made these observations: "Technically, you do better work than I do in my shop. You have better equipment, a better location, and the potential for more clients. But, you have yet to discover you are really in the people business. When you start taking that extra step to get along with others, everything will fall into place." Within one year, a complete turnaround occurred and the business began to operate profitably.

Jennifer was a highly ambitious information manager for a service company. After her boss talked a lot about giving her a substantial raise, but only came through with a small one, she quit. Having discovered that many organizations in her community needed both full and part-time workers on a temporary basis, she opened a "temp" agency. She rented office space, lined up six mature, skilled secretaries and found them assignments in various firms where they quickly and efficiently filled in for others. Jennifer took care of their Social Security deductions, workers' compensation, and unemployment insurance. Her initial clients loved the idea. Today, she has a solid small business operation.

On a local television show, Jennifer was asked to explain her success. She replied: "I make sure I engage skilled workers and treat them right. I follow up to make sure clients understand the system and get their money's worth. More than other kinds of small business operations, I deal 90 percent with human relationships. I'm having a ball and I don't have to depend upon another person for a raise in pay."

Whatever business you are planning to go into, start by analyzing the *people* aspects. In addition to figuring out financial problems, insurance protection, layout schemes, products and services to offer, have a *people plan*.

To get you started in this direction, take a moment to see how much you already know and accept about your people skills:

Your Turn

This exercise is designed to give you some insight into how effective you will be as an entrepreneur in dealing with people. Will you place so much emphasis on the technical side of your business that you neglect the people side? Will you be highly skillful in working with people or will you make avoidable mistakes that will seriously damage your business? Answer the following true and false questions. The correct answers are found at the end of the exercise.

TRUE   FALSE

_____ _____ 1. As the owner of a new business, capital requirements, accounting practices and controls should take precedence over employees and customers.

_____ _____ 2. The decision of whether or not to try to repair a damaged relationship depends upon who is at fault.

TRUE   FALSE

_____ _____   3. Fortunately, the attitude of one employee does not influence the productivity of another.

_____ _____   4. People problems usually take care of themselves.

_____ _____   5. The owner of a small business is also a teacher, counselor, coach, interviewer, supervisor and leader.

_____ _____   6. In starting a new business, the owner should attempt to build a _team_ of full and part-time employees.

_____ _____   7. It is more important for a manager in a large company to delegate responsibilities to employees than it is for a small business owner.

_____ _____   8. Successful business owners prefer to have the respect of team members rather than friendship.

_____ _____   9. Employees who work for small business owners are more trustworthy than those working for large corporations.

_____ _____   10. Keeping employee turnover low is more important than being productive.

_____ _____   11. Fair employment practices do not apply to businesses with five employees or less.

_____ _____   12. It is a mistake for small business operators to employ members of their own family.

_____ _____   13. As an owner, you can terminate an employee with a bad attitude and need not worry about providing documentation.

_____ _____   14. A business owner who considers all workers to be full-fledged _team_ members is in a better position to gain loyalty and productivity than a manager in a giant corporation.

TRUE   FALSE

_____ _____ 15. Building strong relationships with people is the best way to arrive at a profitable bottom line.

_____ _____ 16. A business owner who has daily contact with employees and customers cannot afford to have a negative attitude for a single day.

_____ _____ 17. Entrepreneurs often expect more from their employees than they should.

_____ _____ 18. Entrepreneurs who must start out paying minimum wages to survive can compensate by giving each employee more opportunity to learn.

_____ _____ 19. Full-time employees are more productive than those who work part-time.

_____ _____ 20. People can cause more problems than broken machinery.

TOTAL CORRECT ☐

If you had 16 or more correct answers, you appear to be highly sensitive to human relations. You will probably maintain a good balance between people and technical problems. If you scored between 10 and 16 correct answers, you may need to devote more attention to the people side of your business. If you scored under 10, this may be the most important book you could read in preparing to operate a successful business.

ANSWERS: *1. F 2. F 3. F 4. F 5. T 6. T 7. F 8. T 9. F 10. F 11. F 12. F 13. F 14. T 15. T 16. T 17. T 18. T 19. F 20. T*

IT IS EASY TO MAKE SERIOUS
PEOPLE MISTAKES

Some entrepreneurs are careless about the way they deal with people. Thus, they quickly make damaging mistakes. Broken relationships are most difficult to restore. Awareness, developed through advanced planning, can prevent mistakes similar to those listed below:

► Employing a capable worker without making a character check and only later discovering that the individual is dishonest

► Making an enemy instead of a supporter out of a customer by being stubborn about an insignificant matter

► Victimizing yourself and your business by destroying a relationship with a difficult supplier whose product you need

► Taking a high-producing employee for granted until you are shocked by his or her resignation

Today, more than ever before, the people side of any new business deserves a great deal of attention. More laws protect workers. The cultural mix of the workforce is changing. New skills are required to get higher productivity from people. And workers are better informed about employment practices.

All new entrepreneurs will make mistakes. The thing to remember is that many broken relationships can be repaired. It is only when a business owner neglects to pay attention to people issues that failure usually follows.

TIME MANAGEMENT AND
PEOPLE PROBLEMS

Time management is an important aspect of successfully operating a small business. You would be wise to ask how much of your time will be devoted to people demands such as recruiting, interviewing, training, handling problems and so forth. Depending upon how people-oriented your business is, you can anticipate spending up to 50 percent of your total time on people concerns. If you become highly skillful at preventing human problems and at handling them when they surface, you might cut this time in half. The point is that you will probably devote more time to people problems than you currently anticipate.

How successful you will be with the human dimension of your business may depend, to some extent, on your background. For example, if you have held down a personnel job—interviewing, training, evaluating employees—you naturally have a slight advantage. Or, if you have been a successful manager or supervisor—delegating, counseling, motivating, inspiring—you have a definite edge over anyone without those skills. The combination of both personnel experiences and management seems ideal for being ready to deal with people problems in your own business.

But what if your experiences have been 90 percent technical? What if you have had little preparation in counseling and people management? Will this put you at a disadvantage? The answer is "yes," but only at the beginning. With this book and other sources of help, you can quickly learn the people skills.

Human relations mistakes are easy to make. Even those individuals with management backgrounds make them. Unfortunately, many technically oriented owners only become human relations savvy by making mistakes and correcting them. Most of the time, their businesses survive; sometimes they do not. If you come from a technical background with minimum people experience, your goal should be to take the human side of business seriously. You will reduce your vulnerability by making preparations ahead of time.

THE CHALLENGE IS STIMULATING

When you think of a large corporation, you start at the top with the Chief Executive Officer and then list the many staff specialists. Three *people roles* quickly come into play. First is the Human Resources Director, responsible for the employment and training of personnel and the policies that govern them. Second is the Sales Manager, often part of the marketing department and responsible for building and keeping client relationships. Third are the Purchasing Agents (manufacturing) or Buyers (retail chains), responsible for purchasing supplies or re-sale items.

In your small business you will be the CEO *and* you will play many other roles including Chief Finance Officer and Quality Control Officer. You will also be your own Human Resources Director, Sales Manager and Purchasing Agent.

The good news lies in the challenge your position presents. You can, and should, say to yourself: "I can use everything I have ever learned up to this point in my own business. The opportunities are endless. And, best of all, I can put it all together my way."

Below are some of the basic people challenges you face as an entrepreneur. Place a check mark in the box opposite the five areas where you need the most help.

❑ Talking things over with problem employees—counseling—so they become productive, cooperative workers

❑ Selecting the best job applicants, using acceptable interviewing techniques

❑ Learning to delegate, to free myself to perform more important functions

❑ Following the new mandated rules on discrimination, harassment and employee treatment

❑ Discovering how to set and maintain an *authority line* that is comfortable for employees and prevents them from taking advantage of me

- ❏ Learning the true meaning of empowerment, so that I assist my employees in reaching their potentials and in contributing more to productivity

- ❏ Developing the skills involved in building a team and maintaining healthy relationships with employees, customers, partners and outside professionals

- ❏ Becoming a strong leader who my employees will respect and follow

The rest of this book is devoted to specific techniques and ideas that give you an edge in dealing with employees, customers and suppliers. Follow the suggestions—once your business is off the ground and successful, you will hear: "There are many reasons for your success, but the way you have gained the respect of people must surely be your most spectacular achievement."

ASK YOURSELF

► In operating your own business, will you find it a problem to be the chief financial *and* personnel officer at the same time? If so, discuss your plans to maintain the appropriate balance.

► If you do not consider yourself a people person, how will you make the necessary adjustments?

► Many beginning entrepreneurs learn to be human relations smart through their mistakes. Describe your willingness to learn people skills in advance, so you will not have to make too many mistakes.

CHAPTER TWO

IT ALL
BEGINS
WITH
ATTITUDE

YOU CANNOT PLAY THE GAME ALONE

Attitude is the way you look at things *mentally*—the focus you have on life. In this book, we are concerned with your attitude toward the people side of operating your business. How do you perceive your role as an entrepreneur? Do you see yourself as a person who sits in an office controlling things? Do you also view yourself as a coach, counselor and teacher?

Many small business operators like to compare their operations to playing a game. This is an excellent attitude to assume, because it defines work as something fun to do. When you consider it as a game, you forget that you may be working fifty or sixty hours a week. You recognize that other people can help you win the game—you cannot play the game alone. You own the business, but you eventually need a *team* to win the game.

In this chapter, we will compare entrepreneurship to playing baseball. This approach will assist you in forming a successful attitude. Study the baseball diamond illustrated below. After we reach each base, you will have a chance to express how you intend to play the game. You need not be a baseball fan to enjoy and learn from this analogy.

The way to get on *first base* is to view owning your business as an adventure—not as a job, not as a responsibility, but as an adventure. To get to *second base*, you need to want to be in control. That is, picture yourself at the wheel of a sloop or at the controls of an airplane. To make it to *third base,* focus on being a coach, and build yourself a winning team. You get to *home base* and score a run when you put all the elements together. To continue the baseball analogy, we will look at each base and how to reach it.

First Base: View Entrepreneurship as a Game

Most successful small business operators are risk-takers. In fact, they get a thrill out of taking calculated risks. Their attitude is: "If you don't take chances, you and your business will stagnate. A business is a dynamic organization that must adapt to change and stay on the move. This involves taking risks."

Get Around the Bases and Your Business Succeeds

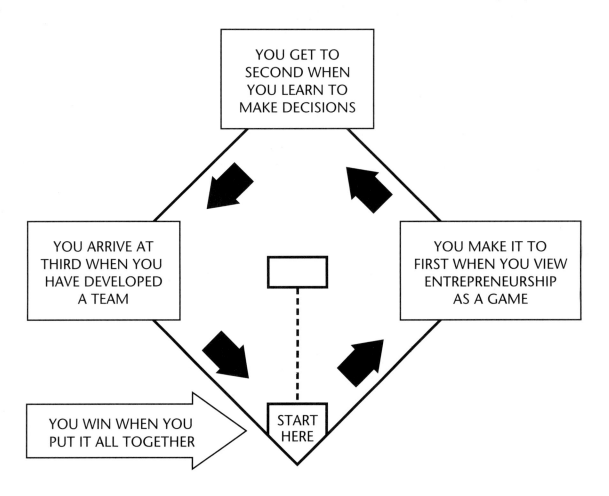

YOU GET TO
SECOND WHEN
YOU LEARN TO
MAKE DECISIONS

YOU ARRIVE AT
THIRD WHEN YOU
HAVE DEVELOPED
A TEAM

YOU MAKE IT TO
FIRST WHEN YOU VIEW
ENTREPRENEURSHIP
AS A GAME

YOU WIN WHEN YOU
PUT IT ALL TOGETHER

START
HERE

Leo has always perceived his repair business as a game he wants to play. Each day, he starts from scratch and winds up winning the game or losing it. Each day, he has the opportunity to satisfy customers, improve his service, streamline his operation, and lock the door feeling he has played well.

Leo figures he has really won if, at the end of each month, his P&L shows a profit. Leo likes to make money. But he views what he does as an adventure. There is excitement, small defeats, problems and a sense of achievement. You cannot win every day, but you can keep the pennant in view. It is Leo's upbeat attitude, day in and day out, that makes him a successful entrepreneur.

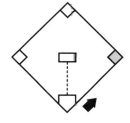

Your Turn   ***Answer the following:***

► Do you like the idea of viewing running your small business as a game? ❑ *Yes* ❑ *No*

► Would this attitude help you become more successful? ❑ *Yes* ❑ *No*

► Would making a game out of your business help you treat people more like a coach does? ❑ *Yes* ❑ *No*

Second Base: Learn to Make Decisions

Many people do not like to make decisions. They would rather follow than lead. Not so with small business operators. They like being up to bat! Entrepreneurs know that they do not bat over 500 when it comes to making decisions. And they also know that they can rectify poor decisions by making good *big* decisions, which help them forget their bad *small* decisions. Even the best hitter in a baseball league frequently walks back to the dugout without having hit even a foul ball.

EXAMPLE

Roberta opened her travel agency because she was tired of having other people make decisions for her. She wants to demonstrate that she is capable and can play hard-ball. Roberta expresses her attitude in these words: "I have come to the conclusion that to get the most out of life, it is best to consider it a game. This way, you may win or lose, but at least you are in charge. Playing the game seems to bring out the best in me. I like being in charge of people, I like showing those who work for me how to deal with difficult customers, solve a computer problem, or deal with an airline rep. Most of all, I enjoy the competition. When I have a highly profitable month, it restores my positive attitude and I'm ready to try again."

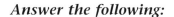

Your Turn   ***Answer the following:***

▶ Do you feel making the right decisions is the best way to get to second base? ❑ *Yes* ❑ *No*

▶ List five other abilities that should be included:

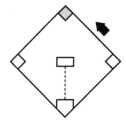

Third Base: Turn a Group of Average Employees into a Motivated Team

You are playing the entrepreneurial game well when you view your challenge as an adventure and make decisions enthusiastically. Getting to third base also takes a lot of finesse in working with people. An excellent way to do this is to have the attitude of a *coach,* as well as that of an employer. Being a coach is more fun than being a boss. The new entrepreneur has all of the advantages of a team leader. When the team wins, the coach—team leader—in a triumphant display of success, is sometimes carried on the shoulders of the players.

As we all know, cohesive teams usually produce more than a group of independent players.

When Jacque opened his nursery, his ex-boss, a corporate vice president, wished him luck and suggested he be a coach to his employees—in somewhat the same manner as he had as coach for the Little League sponsored by the corporation. Jacque took the suggestion to heart and in three years he had a winning team of eight players working for him. Some were in the flower shop, others were out in the field. It was a close group that competed in a highly effective manner with other nurseries in the county.

Jacque expresses his attitude this way: "I'd rather consider myself as a coach than a boss. Of course, I have to correct a few players now and then, but almost all of the time they discipline themselves and play to win. And every time we reach a new goal, we celebrate with a victory dinner."

Your Turn   ***Answer the following:***

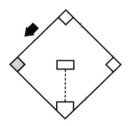

▶ Are you a *natural* team leader? ❑ *Yes* ❑ *No*

▶ Do you understand *group dynamics*? ❑ *Yes* ❑ *No*

▶ List five of the main ingredients to forming a successful small business team.

Home Base: Score by Putting It All Together

To win games and be at the top of the league, you have to put everything together. It takes good pitching, great defense and players with the will to win. Operating a successful business is similar. As the owner, you have to put it all together. This means keeping the financial side of the business in good order—maintaining proper controls, reports and enough cash flow to survive and make improvements. It means keeping production high, while maintaining quality—keeping up with the best equipment and techniques in the industry. It means creating and following a topflight sales and marketing strategy—keeping key clients satisfied and new customers coming in the door. It also means keeping track of government regulations and making sure you comply with current laws, which requires a lot of coordinating and follow-through. Even though you may have done a superior job of getting to first, second and third bases, getting home is not a "piece of cake." All of your management skills must come into play at just the right time.

EXAMPLE

When Katja completed beauty college, she had no idea that within ten years she would own a beauty salon with ten stations. What has been her attitude along the way? At first, she wanted to give each client a new, improved image. Later, she became interested in building a large customer base. Finally, she wanted the challenge of her own shop. She got to third base rather quickly; getting home took time, because she had not anticipated all of the financial problems, human conflicts— mainly among operators—and legal requirements she would face.

Today, Katja feels she is on top of things and claims: "For the first time, I feel I have it together, and each month is a new ball game. I'm pleased to be the owner. I like the recognition and the freedom to make decisions. I sometimes think I would like to sell out and start over with a small shop in a new location. I would make fewer mistakes the second time around, and it would still be fun. When you come right down to it, entrepreneurship is a state of mind."

Your Turn

Answer this question:

► List the ten most important elements or factors that go together to make up a successful small business, starting with:

1. Good human relations

Most people have great expectations when they make their decision to start a business. Their positive attitudes release enthusiasm from within and their excitement usually causes them to work night and day. In the long run, their ability to sustain a positive perspective is what counts. Those who convert a very small beginning into a large corporation must maintain positive attitudes through some tough periods.

As you start out on your adventure, keep these three thoughts in mind:

1. Although profit is the way the score is recorded, entrepreneurship is more than making money. Often, a small business turns out to be both a job and a lifestyle. Frequently, as a business grows, it turns out to be an estate that can be left to family members. Much of the time, a successful small business becomes part of the owner's identity—recognition comes from the success of the business.

2. Entrepreneurship is, in essence, an attitude. It is a way of looking at the business world; it is a way of looking at work. Many people who start a business late in their lives say they really should have started their business years before. They believe they would have been able to make more of it, and they would have enjoyed their lives more. They realize that having their own business is a way of life. Although many people overdo it and devote too much time to a personal business, others have found it to be much better than having a routine job for forty years and following and conforming to the directions of others.

3. You and your attitude is what make it happen. If you operate a *mom & pop* business, the attitudes of both you and your spouse are critical to its success. You cannot have one positive and one negative attitude, and make it work. The same is true in a partnership. Statistics show that the large majority of partnerships fail. This is understandable when you consider how difficult it would be to have two vastly different people view a single business in the same way.

ASK YOURSELF

▶ The way you look at entrepreneurship and the operation of your business *is your attitude.* How do you intend to stay positive during the ups and downs of your adventure? If you turned negative, what would you do about it?

▶ How will you be able to recover quickly when you recognize you have made a bad decision? How will you keep from turning negative?

▶ The baseball analogy is designed to give you a bird's eye view of your adventure. Do you agree that only when you put it all together—good financial planning, quality product or service, good human relations, etc.—will you show a profit—score a run? How will you know when all factors are in balance?

CHAPTER
THREE

RECRUITING

AND

INTERVIEWING

CREATE AN ORGANI-ZATION CHART

The first step to take in building your staff is creating an organization chart so you will know how many start-up employees to hire. Should you start with one full-time and two part-time employees? Could you and your spouse do it alone for a few months? Will you need a dozen employees to get into gear?

Once you have your organization chart on paper, you prepare a job description for each position. If you are seeking part or full-time salespeople, write down exactly what the job entails. If you seek a backup person to do almost everything you do, you need a person with different qualifications. The point is that you need to know the qualifications of the job *before* you look for a person to fill it. Do not rush this process.

Your Turn

Complete the following:

The organization I hope to build within my first year of operation is illustrated in the following chart. I have indicated start-up positions I need to fill with a STAR (*). I have numbered those I will fill later in order of importance. Duties to be performed by each position—job description—can be listed on a separate page.

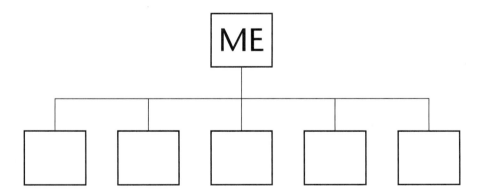

RECRUITING APPLICANTS

Once you complete the organizational chart and know the position or positions you need to fill, you are ready to start the recruitment process. Generally, there are six places to attract applicants for interviews:

1. *Department of Human Resources.* Your local state employment agency can send pre-screened applicants to you for interviewing. It is usually best to contact them in person, so you can be specific about the qualifications you seek.

2. *Private Employment Agencies.* Private agencies, listed in your telephone directory, will screen applicants before they send them to you for interviewing. If you hire one of their referrals, depending on the agency, either you or the applicant pays a fee to the agency.

3. *College Placement Bureaus.* Contact your local universities and community colleges, especially if you seek part-time employees.

4. *Newspaper Want Ads.* Your job descriptions can help you build the best possible ad to attract qualified applicants.

5. *Window Signs.* New retail stores frequently place help-wanted signs in their windows.

6. *Word-Of-Mouth.* Spreading the word among friends, suppliers and neighbors can also generate applicants.

Although it is time consuming, the more applicants that you interview, the better picture you will have as to the quality of local applicants. Interviewing a sizable number of applicants also spreads the word that a new business is opening. Curiosity builds interest, and, if done properly, recruitment is recognized as having good public relations value.

Settle on an appropriate application form as part of the recruiting process—one that gives you the data you need and acts as a screening device. Two sample job application forms are printed on the following pages.

Sample #1 Basic Resume

Personal Data

Name (last, first, middle)   Date

Social Security Number

Address

City   State   Zip code

Home phone (   )   Message Phone (   )

If employed, can you provide proof of U.S. citizenship?   n Yes   n No   n N/A

Are you 18 or over?   n Yes   n No

Position(s) applying for

Referred by

Education Record

High school

Address   Dates attended

Degrees or diplomas

College/University

Address   Dates attended

Degrees or diplomas

Trade or technical training

Address   Dates attended

Degrees or diplomas

Military Service

Branch of service

Dates of service

Duties/special training

Employment History

Begin with most recent employer. Attach additional sheet if needed.

1. Employer   Dates of employment

Address

City   State   Zip code

Phone (   )   Beginning salary   Ending salary

Title/duties

Manager's name

Why did you leave?

2. Employer   Dates of employment

Address

City   State   Zip code

Phone (   )   Beginning salary   Ending salary

Title/duties

Manager's name

Why did you leave?

3. Employer   Dates of employment

Address

City   State   Zip code

Phone (   )   Beginning salary   Ending salary

Title/duties

Manager's name

Why did you leave?

Personal Data

Have you been convicted of a crime (other than traffic violations) or been imprisoned during the last seven years? A conviction will not necessarily bar you from employment.　　　n No　　n Yes

Explain.

Names of friends or relatives that are employed by this company.

Do you have any physical or mental disability that may limit your performance in the job you are applying for? If so, what can be done to accommodate your limitation?

References

List three professional references who are familiar with the quality of your work, have worked directly with you, and have known you at least two years.

1. Reference

Work phone (　　)　　　　　　　　　　　　　Home phone (　　)

Address

City　　　　　　　　　　　State　　　　　　Zip code

Relationship

2. Reference

Work phone (　　)　　　　　　　　　　　　　Home phone (　　)

Address

City　　　　　　　　　　　State　　　　　　Zip code

Relationship

3. Reference

Work phone (　　)　　　　　　　　　　　　　Home phone (　　)

Address

City　　　　　　　　　　　State　　　　　　Zip code

Relationship

Applicant's signature _____ Date _____

Page 3 of 3

Sample #2 Customized Resume

MAIL TO: XYZ Company, Inc.
Street Address
City, State, Zip code

AN EQUAL OPPORTUNITY EMPLOYER
Federal and/or state laws prohibit discrimination based on age; sex;
national origin; race; religion; or marital; veteran or handicap status.

Please Print Clearly   Today's Date _____/ _____/ _____

PERSONAL

Name _____
(First)   (Middle)   (Last)

Address _____ Home Phone _____

City/State/Zip _____ Message No. _____

Have you ever worked or attended school under another name?
_____ No _____ Yes   If Yes, please provide that name: _____

Do you have a valid Driver's License?   _____ No _____ Yes   If Yes, in which state? _____
Social Security No. _____ - _____ - _____

Are you under 18 years old?   _____ No _____ Yes   If Yes, please attach a copy of your work permit.

Are you either a U.S. Citizen or Permanent Resident? _____ Yes _____ If No, please answer the following:
   Do you have the legal right to work? _____ No   _____ Yes
   Visa Type: _____ B1   _____ F1   _____ H1   _____ J1   _____ L1   Other _____

Position Desired _____ Years Related Experience _____

What prompted you to apply at XYZ Company, Inc?

_____ Newspaper Ad   _____ Agency (Name) _____
_____ Employee Referral By _____   _____ Other (specify) _____

Do you have relatives employed at XYZ Company, Inc. ?   _____ No _____ Yes   If Yes, please give their name(s):
_____

What hours do you prefer to work? _____ _____ Full-time _____ Part-time
Are there certain days of the week that you cannot work? _____ No   _____ Yes, list days _____
Can you work overtime?   _____ No _____ Yes

Do you have any condition which may limit your ability to perform the job(s) applied for?
_____ No _____ Yes   If Yes, what can be done to accommodate your limitations?
_____
_____

Have you ever been convicted of a felony?
_____ No _____ Yes   If Yes, give date, place, offense and outcome.
(Previous convictions do not exclude an applicant from
consideration for employment.)

Page 1 of 3

EMPLOYMENT HISTORY

Please list in chronological order all of your work history over the last 10 years, beginning with your most recent job. Information provided on this application may be verified.

PLEASE COMPLETE EVEN IF YOU HAVE SUBMITTED A RESUME.

Employer (Present or Last Company) _____

City, State _____

Your Position or Title _____

Supervisor's Name _____ Phone _____

Your Job Duties _____

_____

Reason for Leaving _____

May we contact your present employer? __ Yes __No

Employed (from/to) _____ / _____

Ending Base Salary $ _____

Base Salary Per   ____ Hour ____Month ____Year
                              (Check one of the above)

Other Compensation _____
(Please explain any additional compensation you received, such as bonuses or commissions.)

Amount of Other Compensation $ _____

Shift Premium _____
        (If you received a shift premium, please show the rate here.)

Former Employer _____

City, State _____

Your Position or Title _____

Supervisor's Name _____ Phone _____

Your Job Duties _____

_____

Reason for Leaving _____

Employed (from/to) _____ / _____

Ending Base Salary $ _____

Base Salary Per   ____ Hour ____Month ____Year
                              (Check one of the above)

Other Compensation _____
(Please explain any additional compensation you received, such as bonuses or commissions.)

Amount of Other Compensation $ _____

Shift Premium _____
        (If you received a shift premium, please show the rate here.)

Former Employer _____

City, State _____

Your Position or Title _____

Supervisor's Name _____ Phone _____

Your Job Duties _____

_____

Reason for Leaving _____

Employed (from/to) _____ / _____

Ending Base Salary $ _____

Base Salary Per   ____ Hour ____Month ____Year
                              (Check one of the above)

Other Compensation _____
(Please explain any additional compensation you received, such as bonuses or commissions.)

Amount of Other Compensation $ _____

Shift Premium _____
        (If you received a shift premium, please show the rate here.)

Former Employer _____

Your Position or Title _____

Former Employer _____

Your Position or Title _____

Employed (from/to) _____ / _____

Reason for Leaving _____

Employed (from/to) _____ / _____

Reason for Leaving _____

EDUCATION

Did you graduate from high school or pass an equivalency exam? _____ Yes _____ No

Please list any college or vocational training in the space below.

School (Name & Location) _____

Degree/Certificate Granted? ____ Yes ____ No Level or Type ____ Dates Attended (from/to) _____/_____

School (Name & Location) _____

Degree/Certificate Granted? ____ Yes ____ No Level or Type ____ Dates Attended (from/to) _____/_____

School (Name & Location) _____

Degree/Certificate Granted? ____ Yes ____ No Level or Type ____ Dates Attended (from/to) _____/_____

REFERENCES

Please list three job or professional references.

Name _____ Title _____ Phone(____) _____

Name _____ Title _____ Phone(____) _____

Name _____ Title _____ Phone(____) _____

PLEASE READ THE FOLLOWING CAREFULLY BEFORE SIGNING

I also understand that XYZ Company, Inc. is a drug-free work place and state that I do not abuse drugs, alcohol or restricted substances.

I also understand the XYZ Company, Inc. needs to verify statements or certain information about me to evaluate my qualification for employment and to conduct its business if I become an employee. Therefore, I authorize the Company to investigate my past employment, educational credentials, and other employment-related statements and activities. I agree to cooperate in such investigations and release those parties supplying information to the Company from all liability or responsibility with respect to information supplied.

I understand that should I be hired, any false answers or statements made by me on this application, and any supplement thereto, or in connection with the above mentioned investigations may result in immediate discharge.

_____   _____
Applicant's Signature   Date

INTERVIEWING APPLICANTS

Most new owners find interviewing applicants to be an enjoyable process. One reason for this is that owners *like* to talk about their new adventures. For best results, certain procedures should be followed. Five of the techniques you will want to follow are listed below:

1. Select a quiet, private location where there will be as few interruptions as possible.

2. Put the applicant at ease, so that you can get fair and realistic reactions.

3. Encourage the applicant to talk through appropriate questions, so you will learn about her or his potential to contribute.

4. Provide the applicant the opportunity to ask questions.

5. Ask applicants if they are willing to accept a trial or probation period, in the event you offer them the job.

Listed below are questions that interviewers typically ask job seekers to generate a dialogue. This ensures that you can base your decision on as much information as possible.

▶ Tell me about yourself.

▶ Why do you want to work here?

▶ What are your skill levels?

▶ Why did you leave your last job?

Take care to ask the same questions of all applicants, so that individuals are given the same opportunity to communicate and, from your point of view, you can make the most objective comparisons. Do not ask questions of a highly personal nature or those that might embarrass or confuse the applicant.

Employment interviews are normally divided into two different approaches. One is the guided pattern or directive approach; the other is a less structured or unguided approach.

A guided interview is often best for an inexperienced interviewer. Consider using a *Job Qualification Checklist,* similar to the one below:

Job Qualification Checklist

	Yes	No
1. Will the applicant work in a cooperative and harmonious way with me and the rest of the staff?	❑	❑
2. Does the applicant have a good work attitude? Does she or he really want to produce?	❑	❑
3. Does the individual have the skills required for the job to be filled?	❑	❑
4. Is the applicant seeking a permanent or interim job? Even if it is a part-time position, you want someone who will stay with you as long as possible.	❑	❑
5. If you seek a part-time employee, will this individual be dependable and stick with the schedule?	❑	❑
6. Does the applicant have a strong learning attitude? That is, will he or she be enthusiastic about learning?	❑	❑

Your Turn

Add two qualifications of your own:

► _____ ❑ ❑

► _____ ❑ ❑

Although no system is perfect, any guided pattern has the advantage of providing at least some objectivity. The goal is to find the most qualified candidate, who will contribute most to the growth of your organization and stay with you for the longest time. Cultural background, gender, age and physical handicaps are not considerations.

EVALUATING APPLICANTS

If you devote an afternoon to interviewing six applicants for a single part-time job, will you talk to enough people to make a good choice? In all probability, the answer is yes. However, if you have not found the most qualified applicant, continue the process. Once you sense that it is time to make a decision, you will need some form of rating system. What should it be? The interview evaluation form below might provide the answer.

Interview Evaluation Form

Job Title _____

Applicant _____ **Telephone** _____

List, in priority order, the skills and characteristics necessary to perform the job. Then, rate each applicant. Use *A* as the top rating, *B* as satisfactory, and *C* as acceptable. A *D* in any category will usually disqualify the applicant.

Required Skills/Characteristics   **Rating**

_____

_____

_____

_____

_____

_____

Total Rating

The interview evaluation form assists you in finding the individual with the best qualifications for the job in question. After you complete a form for each applicant—and make your decision—keep all forms of the applicants on file for legal purposes.

CHECKING REFERENCES

Make a reference check before you call back your best applicant for a second, and perhaps final, interview. If the applicant has recently left another job, a telephone call to the previous employer is appropriate. If yours would be the applicant's first job, you might call the local high school or college. All you need to do is give them your name, explain that you are opening a new business and thinking about employing an ex-employee or student. Ask for verification of employment or attendance. Follow up by asking for further information on the applicant's performance. If you only receive verification data, do not press the point; to avoid possible litigation, some employers have a policy of only providing employment dates.

If everything seems in order, call the most qualified applicant for a second interview. Ask the individual if she or he will accept employment on a trial basis. If you get a *yes* answer, congratulate the applicant, go over salary and other details, and ask the individual to report for work at a specified time for further consultation and orientation.

FOUR HIRING MISTAKES YOU DO NOT WANT TO MAKE

1. If there are other, equally qualified applicants, avoid hiring someone who is currently working through a major personal problem. Although the individual may be qualified, the personal problem may overshadow the possibility of producing at an acceptable level.

Mrs. Drake has all of the skills necessary for being the kind of employee you seek. During the interview, however, she confided that she is going through a difficult divorce, has two teenagers over which she has lost control, and her doctor has advised her against working more than twenty hours per week. Despite Mrs. Drake's technical competency, her personal circumstances are likely to interfere with her performance.

2. Never enter into an employment agreement without discussing a "trial period." Explain that the policy benefits both parties, so you can evaluate each other; the final decision can be made by either party, on or before a specified date.

3. Avoid tokenism. Provide equal consideration and opportunities for all qualified minority applicants.

4. Try not to over-identify with an applicant, to the point you show favoritism. Interviewers are sometimes so *taken* by a part-time applicant that they allow their bias or a favorable first impression to over-influence their better judgment.

EXAMPLE

A few months ago, Julie, a professional interviewer, hired a foreign student who charmed her into throwing away the rules. Yesterday, the store detective discovered the part-timer had established a ring of other employees who were stealing merchandise and selling it, off hours, in a flea market.

Your Turn   **This chapter has presented the bare essentials to the employment process. Adapt what you have learned to your own situation. One way to do this is to conduct a mock interview. That is, have a friend or family member go through the process of applying for the job in question so that you can make the applicant feel at ease, ask appropriate questions, fill out the** Interview Evaluation Form, **and "get the hang" of how you will proceed with real applicants.**

ASK YOURSELF

► Do you agree with the statement "an organization is only as good as the people who operate it"? If so, describe your plans to select your staff in a manner that guarantees that you will start out with the best people available for each position.

► Describe the public relations value to setting up a smooth, friendly and fair employment process.

► Discuss the results of a small business owner employing people "by the seat of his pants."

CHAPTER FOUR

ORIENTATION OF THE NEW EMPLOYEE

THE BEST HUMAN INVEST- MENT

The best opportunity you have to build a good, solid working relationship with your employees is when you first hire them. Research shows that employees treated right at the beginning become better producers, stay longer and remain loyal. The best way to build a winning *team* is to give each new employee enough personal time during his or her orientation. It is the best human investment you can make.

ORIENTATION GOALS

What should be your goals in providing the best orientation possible for each new employee? Here are three:

▶ Gain the highest degree of productivity from the employee, in the shortest period of time.

▶ Build a healthy, two-way relationship with the employee—one that will, hopefully, last a long time and motivate the individual to make a major contribution to your business.

▶ Assist the employee in becoming an enthusiastic *team* player under your leadership, so that the success of your business is important to the individual.

For best results, you may wish to divide your new employees' orientation into these seven steps:

SEVEN STEPS TO A BETTER ORIENTATION

Step 1: Give the new employee a clear picture of what lies ahead. Anxiety usually has a firm grip on new employees. They want to know what to expect, how to behave and what their work will be. Take the time to sit down and give them a chance to know you and to ask questions. Make them feel as important as they are to the future of your business.

After her first day on the job as a part-timer, LaVoy decided she really liked the work and that it would be a perfect set-up until she graduated from the university in four years. She made a firm commitment to herself to do her best, learn all she could and stick with it.

How did things work out? Four years later, after receiving her degree, LaVoy used the part-time work experience—she became a fill-in manager—in her resume. The owner also wrote her an outstanding letter of reference. She had helped to support herself through college, and she had prepared herself for her career.

Step 2: Give them all the job details. Every job has rules and perimeters. Look over the orientation form that follows. Select items you feel it is important to cover in your operation. Give the new employee this form and having him or her sign it and return a copy to you is a good idea.

Step 3: Cover the job responsibilities. At this point, it is a good idea to talk about the job itself. What are you looking for in the way of performance? What is your policy toward customers? Tell the employee that he or she will be given detailed data by you or a *sponsor* later. Explain that, generally speaking, you desire certain behaviors. Above all, you want the new employee to be happy and enjoy his or her job.

Step 4: Take the employee for a tour. Any orientation should include a *walk around* the facility. Introduce the individual to other members of the staff, locate the rest rooms, the employee *coffee* areas, parking places, etc. Be receptive to questions and get the employee to relax before you move into your training program. The hypothetical *Memorandum* on page 44 may give you some additional ideas on orientation.

Step 5: Provide an opportunity for the employee to ask questions. A primary purpose of orientation is to help new employees feel comfortable in their new surroundings. Giving them a chance to ask questions helps employees discover more about the business, and it strengthens the relationship between the owner—you—and the individual.

Sample Orientation Form*

Dear _____

We're glad you've joined our organization. As your supervisor takes you through the orientation process, he or she will cover a number of topics. This checklist is provided to ensure you are familiar with all the necessary information. Feel free to ask plenty of questions. We want your entry into our company to be as simple as possible!

_____ Working hours	_____ Attendance policy
_____ Rate of pay	_____ Dress code
_____ Pay period, first pay	_____ Telephone calls
_____ Payroll deductions	_____ Organizational structure
_____ Benefits program	_____ Tour of facility
_____ Medical plan (dates eligible)	_____ Parking
_____ Emergency leave policy	_____ Lunch areas
_____ Work rules	_____ "Buddy" assigned
_____ Job description reviewed	_____ Job evaluation
_____ Discipline procedures	_____ Termination policy
_____ Introductory period	_____ Probation policy

Completed forms: _____ W-4   _____ Personal data form   _____ I-9

_____ Waiver/designation of beneficiary for insurance plans

Special notes _____

_____

I understand these are general guidelines and may be changed at any time as business requires. The information above does not constitute a written contract, and I understand my employment is for no definite period of time and may be ended at will.

I acknowledge that we have discussed all of the above.

_____   _____
Employee signature/date   Supervisor signature/date

*Reprinted with permission from *High Performance Hiring* by Robert W. Wendover, Crisp Publications, Inc. Menlo Park, CA 94025.

Memorandum

Here are a few ideas on how we can make the most of orienting new employees:

- Meet the employee at the front desk.

- Provide a brief history of the organization, including mission, organizational chart, products, position in the industry or field and anything you deem important.

- Give an organizational tour. Go into some depth, but not too much. Encourage questions and get to know the person on a personal level.

- Explain your department's function within the organization. What role does it play? How is it related to others? What departments are dependent on it? On what departments does it depend?

- Review the job description. Cover duties, authority, relationships with others in the department. Make sure this information is understood.

- Discuss attendance, tardiness, sickness, vacation and hours of work.

- Complete I-9, benefit and payroll forms.

- Introduce buddy. (Match this person with someone in your department to assist him/her in adjusting to new surroundings. Give it some thought and select a buddy ahead of time.)

- Introduce this person to the staff member conducting training. If you will be conducting the training, set the schedule.

- In general, get all new hires involved in the department as soon as possible and make them feel at home and needed.

Reprinted with permission from *High Performance Hiring* by Robert W. Wendover, Crisp Publications, Inc. Menlo Park, CA 94025.

Step 6: Spell out the learning opportunities. New employees want to feel they have made the right decision when they accept a job. Explain that their job will increase their knowledge and better prepare them for the future, no matter where they go or what they do. For example, if the job includes customer contact, the employee will learn how to deal with difficult customers and will be better prepared for future human relationships of all kinds.

Step 7: Continuously follow-up. As busy as you may be, keep in touch with new employees as much as possible. For example, you will have made a smart move if you can spend ten minutes with them at the end of each day for a week. If you cannot have daily contact during the first week, have a single meeting at the end of the week. Ask "how are things going?" Discuss his or her progress and what needs to be accomplished during the following week.

Your Turn   *From your experience, what you have read in the past few pages, and as is appropriate for the business you are building, outline below the orientation program you will put into operation. Answer such questions as:*

▶ Will you present the orientation yourself?

▶ How long will you spend?

▶ Will you use any printed materials?

▶ What kind of follow-up will you provide?

WHEN A NEW EMPLOYEE DOES NOT WORK OUT

In preparing and executing a rewarding orientation plan, you must recognize that not all the people you hire will work out. Some will not find you or the type of work you provide up to their expectations. A few may not be capable of reaching close enough to your standards. Under these conditions the employee should be relieved, for the benefit of both parties.

Krikor gave Inga the best possible orientation, but from the start he wondered if he had made a mistake when he hired her. She did not have the personal confidence to meet and deal with his sophisticated clients. Still, after her two-week probation period was over, Krikor did not have the heart to release Inga and help her find a different job where she would be more successful.

Krikor and Inga both did their best to make the arrangement work; after three months, Krikor finally sat down and discussed the problem with her. During the three months that had elapsed, Inga had been unhappy and Harvey had been less effective as the owner.

Both agreed to terminate the relationship. When the termination arrangements were complete, Inga relaxed and felt much better. Krikor told himself: "Next time, when I can tell during orientation that a new employee won't make it, I'm going to have the courage to terminate the individual at the end of the probation period. After all, that is why I set up a trial period in the first place."

ASK YOURSELF

▶ Explain why a good orientation program is important to you.

▶ Discuss why it is equally important to provide part-timers with a good orientation as it is full-timers.

▶ Describe your ability to admit you have made a hiring mistake, and to terminate an individual, either before or at the close of the probation period.

CHAPTER
FIVE

TRAINING

YOUR

STAFF

THE FIRST THIRTY DAYS

It normally takes a new employee about thirty days to become fully oriented and to absorb the training necessary to do a highly productive job. It is helpful to provide the new employee with a way to assess his or her progress each week, and then arrange a meeting with a supervisor for a thirty-day evaluation, prior to achieving regular employment status.

Research indicates that almost *all* employees are anxious to learn. Many have great learning attitudes. They recognize that no matter how much formal education they may have had, learning on the job is different and exciting. Younger employees often place learning above monetary rewards.

What does this mean to you, the new business owner? It means you have a great opportunity to bring in young, eager minds that are ready and anxious to learn and *perform* within your business. *All you need to do is provide the right kind of training.*

SEVEN STEPS TO MORE EFFECTIVE TRAINING

How do you go about providing this training? Will you, personally, have time to do it? How important is training to the future of your enterprise? Here are seven steps that you might consider:

Step 1: Assign a sponsor. Give each new employee an experienced person to work with, until the required job skills are mastered. The sponsor can be someone already on your payroll, or it can be you. The larger your organization becomes, the less time you may have to do the training yourself.

Rose got her first job in an ice cream/cookie store, before she entered college. She was fortunate that the owner of the store devoted one full morning to training her in all aspects of her job. Before the day was over, she had started to build her confidence in dealing with customers. Now, in her senior year in college, Rose still returns during holiday periods to work as a night manager in the store.

In many respects, formal education is designed to give the student the tools for learning. On-the-job training takes advantage of this learning potential. Whatever your business, it will require many special skills that can be taught only at the workstation. When these skills are taught patiently, one step at a time, with an opportunity for the employee to ask questions, he or she learns and your business profits. Without the right kind of training, the learner becomes discouraged, and you become unhappy with the individual's performance. Both parties lose.

Step 2: Recommend campus training if it is available.
Frequently, a new employee has all of the qualifications for a given job, with the exception of one competency. When this occurs, taking an on-campus class may be the answer.

EXAMPLE

It was obvious from his first day on the job that James would make an outstanding employee if he could quickly upgrade his computer skills. The solution? Augment his on-the-job learning with more formal training each night, on campus. The result? James did so well with his double learning approach that he decided to continue his on-campus learning when it was no longer required at work.

Many large corporations pay full or partial fees to encourage their workers to upgrade their knowledge. Although, as a small beginning business, this may not be advisable, do everything you can to encourage learning from all sources, even if this means losing the employee to a better job somewhere else in the future.

Step 3: Provide employees with self-help materials.
Whatever your type of business may be, there are probably training materials available to help new employees. Some can

be found at a local library, other material can be purchased and used over and over with each new employee hired. For example, a single copy of the book *Your First Thirty Days* by Crisp Publications could be purchased and re-used to help each new employee become productive sooner.

When Grace hired Bonita as a salesperson in her high fashion dress shop, she knew that Bonita had never received any sales training. She recognized, however, that Bonita had all the other qualities required and that, with help, Bonita would soon be an expert. Grace's first step was to ask Bonita to read a book on sales-manship that Grace used when starting her shop; her second step was to have Bonita observe Grace's selling techniques. The result? In less than a month, Bonita was doing an excellent job.

Step 4: Follow up so both parties are happy with results. Unfortunately, you cannot do a little training at the beginning and expect top performance from then on. You must continue to check on the progress of the employee. Training is a continuous project. For example, if you are doing the training yourself, when you finish with the basics you will want to check back—the same or the following day, in a week and after thirty days. You may even want to conduct a formal review before you grant permanent status.

After Adam had devoted more than a week to training Hakim as a swimming pool maintenance expert, he turned him loose on his own. Adam asked Hakim to check in with him each night to discuss problems and to ask questions. At the end of two weeks, Adam knew that Hakim could handle the job, but he still waited thirty days and made a few surprise inspections before his training program was over.

Step 5: Rotate assignments. In a small business, employees are typically asked to perform a wide variety of tasks. Specialization, at the beginning, is impossible. The more you can rotate jobs among your staff, the better. Rotation provides training in more directions, curtails boredom, and prepares employees to take over tasks when co-workers are absent.

Step 6: Give credit and recognition. Surveys show that most managers in large firms do not pay enough compliments. The same may be true of small business owners. Many are so busy with demands from many directions, they fail to give recognition when an employee learns a new task or performs an old one with a high level of efficiency.

Step 7: Make on-the-job learning a continuous experience for your employees. As you develop, refine and expand your business, do not leave your staff behind. *Let them grow along with you.* Where possible, stick with the promotion-from-within policy which will, in effect, be a measure of your success in training your people. If you can promote your own people as your business develops, you know that your training program is working.

Large corporations have complete training departments, large budgets and sophisticated programs. The small business person must weave the training of new employees into an already busy schedule. It is an important function that cannot be neglected.

How Good Are You at Training Others?*

Are you an effective trainer? Your attitude, knowledge and approach will influence what is learned and how well it is applied. Here are some suggestions to improve the return on investment in training for all concerned.

Place a ✓ if you already do what is suggested and an ✗ if you plan to begin this practice.

❑ 1. Review performance against expectations with each employee periodically, and jointly identify training that will strengthen results.

❑ 2. Listen to an employee's growth objectives, and support them when it is appropriate to do so.

❑ 3. Talk in advance to employees selected for training, to reinforce the importance of the training to their job.

❑ 4. Have an employee's work covered by others during training, so she or he can concentrate on what is being taught.

❑ 5. Help employees develop an action plan to apply their training to their jobs.

❑ 6. Ask the employees to evaluate the training program and whether it would be suitable for other members of the team.

❑ 7. Assign work to employees that allows them to apply new techniques and methods learned during training.

❑ 8. Compliment employees when they apply their newly acquired skills.

*Reprinted with permission from *Team Building: An Exercise in Leadership* by Robert B. Maddux, Crisp Publications, Inc., 1200 Hamilton Court, Menlo Park, CA 94025.

Your Turn **Outline below your training plans for your operation:**

► Will you do the training yourself at the start?

► When will you assign the responsibility to another person?

► What kind of training will be required?

► What outside materials might you use?

► What kind of follow-up will be appropriate?

Keep in mind that the best way to build a sound, lasting business relationship is to teach an employee how to do something skillfully that he or she have never performed in the past.

APPRAISING EMPLOYEE PERFORMANCE

Sooner or later it will be smart to set up an appraisal system to evaluate your employees on their performance. You have three options. You can:

1. Take a more informal approach and sit down with all of your employees once a year, or every six months, and discuss their progress. This way you do not need to develop a standard form of your own or to copy one.

2. Follow a formal appraisal system, using a standard form as used by large organizations, and tie the results to any salary increases you decide to provide.

3. Develop a short appraisal form of your own, and tie any salary increases or bonuses to the performance rating.

Adopt one of the above options; employees *want to know how they are doing.* Without a system and a regular schedule for performance ratings, you may neglect this kind of significant two-way communication. If you start your business with only a handful of employees, you may opt at the start for an informal system; later, as your organization expands, you may graduate into a more formal system.

ASK YOURSELF

▶ Is the orientation of new employees more important than the training that follows? Or, are both functions equally important?

▶ What are the long-range human relation implications for the small entrepreneur who has a strong—or weak— training program?

▶ Many small business owners claim that they prefer to train new employees themselves. They say it is the best way to build team spirit. Are you willing to commit yourself to this function?

CHAPTER SIX

FIVE MAGICAL FOUNDATIONS

THE BASIC PRINCIPLES

At one time, I taught courses on how to be a good supervisor. Years later, in San Antonio, Texas, I ran into a man who had taken the course. I accepted his invitation to join him for dinner at his favorite restaurant.

During dinner, he commented, "You may not remember, but in your course you gave what you claimed to be five irreplaceable foundations, as far as being a good owner-manager is concerned. Well, I took you seriously. Two or three years after taking your course, I started a business of my own, on very little capital, an average location, and not enough experience. But, ahead of everything else, I put your five foundations into practice. In fact, I called them my *human relations credo* and built my entire philosophy on how to work with employees around them. I continue to follow them to this very day."

Later in the evening, he asked me how I liked the restaurant. After an evening of imported wine, superior food, outstanding service and a comfortable ambiance, I told him it was the best meal I had enjoyed in weeks. "Wonderful!" he replied, "This was my first restaurant. I now own seven others like it around the state."

The *irreplaceable* foundations that my ex-student used successfully to build his business constitute the body of this chapter. While the material has been brought up-to-date, the basic principles remain the same.

FOUNDATION 1: Let People Know How They Are Doing

When people ask me, "How are you doing?" my stock reply is: "I have no idea, because nobody tells me." I am joking, of course, but there is a touch of truth in my answer. Small business operators are so busy, they frequently forget to tell individuals on their team how they are doing. This is a major mistake.

Assume for a moment that you have neglected telling your *gang* how they are doing. How could you make amends? You could call an informal staff meeting and share some sales or production figures that would make everyone feel better. Or, you could approach each individual on a one-on-one basis and make comments such as these:

> *"Marta, you may be interested in how you are doing, from my perspective. Well, you are probably doing better than you think. I am very pleased with your progress, and happy you are a member of this team."*

> *"Gunnar, I know you are probably still upset about the mistake you made last week, but if you stacked all the good things you have done since we started this business beside that one mistake, it would be, and is, insignificant. If it is important for you to know, I think you are doing well in your job and I would hate to lose you."*

> *"I am sorry to hear that you do not feel you are making as big a contribution to our team as you want to make. If you could see the progress you have made from a distance, as I do, you would feel much better about yourself. You are doing a good job and you'll be doing better and better as you continue to learn."*

We all have a basic, inner need to know how we are doing in life. Not many people are in a position to tell us. When you own a business, you will get higher productivity from your people when you let them know how they are doing—even when they are doing poorly, they need to know.

FOUNDATION 2: Pay Some Hidden or Unexpected Compliments

In essence, this suggestion means to give credit to someone for an isolated or infrequent incident of good behavior. For example, someone working for you might be in a slump. Rather than jumping on this person, do the opposite. Seek and find something the individual has done that is deserving of a compliment—even if it is hidden under many examples of negative behavior.

In the past, Sally has been the most valuable salesperson in your small shop. Recently, however, you have received complaints about her. You have also noticed that Sally is less enthusiastic with co-workers. Should you call her in for counseling?

Unsure how to approach this delicate situation, you search for a hidden compliment. Then, while on the selling floor assisting a long-time customer, you discover that normally she prefers to be served by Sally who, in the past, has been extremely sensitive to her needs. Later that day, you call Sally into your office and relate the kind words the customer had for her. You also tell Sally that you deeply appreciate having her on your staff and that you wish to do everything possible to keep her happy.

The hidden compliment idea—some people call it reverse psychology—is designed to give employees who are temporarily *down*, a lift. It can be used on employees, customers, suppliers and professionals such as your CPA or lawyer. Paying such compliments, of course, does not mean you should cut back on giving credit when it is due to those who are *not* having trouble with their attitudes. It simply means that you may have someone on your staff who desperately needs a compliment to feel better about her or himself.

Your Turn   **In the space below, write the name of someone—an employee, friend or family member—to whom you intend to pay a hidden compliment in the next few days.**

FOUNDATION 3: Be Generous With Your Expertise

As the owner of a small business, you have three ways to express your leadership—through your role as owner, through your personality, and *by sharing your knowledge with your staff*. The more time you take to share your knowledge, the stronger the relationships you build will be.

When Marge opened her flower shop, she spent many hours helping Ramona understand the basics of designing an attractive floral piece. With her native Hispanic artistic talent, Ramona became outstanding at her craft. That was eight years ago. Looking back on what has made her business so successful, Marge admits the time devoted to training Ramona was the key. Recently, Ramona remarked: "I will never forget how patient you were with me, in sharing your knowledge. It is the main reason I have been so happy working with you all these years. You earned my loyalty from the very beginning."

The demands on the owner of a small business are so great that it is difficult to squeeze out time to train inexperienced employees. Yet, it can be the best investment you can make. Sharing your knowledge will do more to build a strong, loyal, permanent relationship than increasing pay or benefits, or giving an employee extra time off.

Only you know just how you want to operate your business. This means you must assume responsibility of training others to do their jobs the right way. If you are generous with your knowledge, you will reap many extra dividends.

FOUNDATION 4: Involve Your Team In Decision-Making

Many profit-making entrepreneurs are well organized, fast moving individuals who are capable of making good decisions. Many have an excellent decision-making track record. Because of this, many have a tendency to make quick decisions without involving their staff or team members. This is often a mistake.

Mozelle, the owner of a successful fashion boutique in a small town, had been paying a free-lance display specialist to build a new front window display twice each month. When the professional left town, Mozelle was at a loss as to where she might locate a replacement. The solution? She decided to ask her one full-time and two part-time employees what to do.

They suggested that she rotate the task among them. After three months, Mozelle had to admit that not only were the displays better, all three salespeople had become more motivated. Sales increased, enabling Mozelle to provide a Christmas bonus for each employee.

It is an excellent policy to turn over appropriate problems to the people who work for you. Let them struggle with a few solutions, even when you can find the answers alone. When they are involved in helping you make a decision, they are apt to support it with enthusiasm. And, as was true with Jennifer, their decision may be better than yours. If so, give them credit.

Involving staff members in solutions should never be a *token* involvement. If they discover you doing what you intended to do all along, your effort will be considered *plastic;* it will have done more harm than good. Involving employees in the decision-making process is the best way to build a *team* that will give your operation a competitive edge.

Do it with an open mind and do it often!

FOUNDATION 5: Be Accessible!

In many small business ventures, owners and employees are thrown physically close together. This facilitates building a team and makes accessibility easy. In addition, many owners mix with employees in performing tasks and dealing with customers. But being accessible—available—is more than being physically present. It is 90 percent attitude.

This means that you are not only close at hand to talk to, but you also *welcome* conversations that deal with problems, complaints and suggestions. In other words, you communicate an attitude that says, "I am willing to listen to you at any time. Do not be afraid to discuss any subject that will improve this business. I respect your judgment. I need your help."

EXAMPLE

Kim and Yoshi opened their dry cleaning operation last year. Both have trouble with the English language. Kim is making faster progress than Yoshi. Although the business is producing greater income than they had anticipated, their three employees—all part-timers—hesitate to discuss problems with the owners. This is especially true with Yoshi, who seems aloof and distant.

Sensing the problem, Kim invited Jane, the most outspoken of the three employees, to lunch. Jane suggested that Kim make it a policy to discuss problems openly, and represent both herself and her husband. After their conversation, Kim made herself accessible and communication barriers were eliminated.

Operating a business requires that the owner spend hours planning, keeping accounts, ordering supplies and working in a *backroom*. The technical side of any successful business is demanding. But the human side of business can also get an owner into deep trouble. To know what your staff or team is thinking, to understand what keeps them productive, and to create a working environment that is conducive to a *team* operation requires constant communication on many subjects, with all employees. This can only happen when you make yourself accessible.

Your Turn

If you currently own a small business, list ways in which you intend to make yourself more accessible to your employees.

Now that you have been introduced to the five magical foundations, you may be saying, "They are just common sense!" It is true—they do not constitute theories that are difficult to understand. In fact, it is *because* they are so easy to understand that you may underestimate their value in building your business. Do not permit this to happen. You can do two things right now to make sure you weave them into your personal behavior patterns and give your venture a better chance of succeeding:

Your Turn

Prioritize the five foundations. That is, list them according to their importance to your operation.

1.

2.

3.

4.

5.

Transfer what you have written above to a small billfold-size card. Use this as a constant reminder of how you can build good relationships with your staff.

ASK YOURSELF

▶ Which of the five magical foundations will be the most difficult for you to maintain? Why?

▶ How can you train yourself to consistently use *all five* foundations?

▶ Have you worked for someone who failed to use the five foundations? Why, in your opinion, did he or she permit this?

CHAPTER
SEVEN

UNDERSTANDING
PRODUCTIVITY

THE HUMAN SIDE OF PRODUC- TIVITY

Personal productivity is the amount and quality of work performed by an individual during a specific period of time. *Group productivity* is the amount and quality of work performed by a team or department of employees in a specific period of time. Productivity in some jobs (e.g., assembly lines) is easily measured. In other jobs (e.g., secretarial), it is more difficult, because so many factors (e.g., telephone efficiency, decision making) are involved. Ultimately, productivity determines who wins in the marketplace. Thus, productivity is the key to meeting and beating competition in a neighborhood, throughout a city and internationally.

Productivity has a human side. For example, the closer those on your payroll live up to their potential, the more successful your operation will be. As a new owner, it is natural to find yourself doing much of the work yourself, *but you cannot do it all.* The more your staff does for you, living up to their potential, the more you will free yourself to live up to yours.

Assume you start your business with five full or part-time employees. The diagram below illustrates the *gap* between what each employee *could* produce and what is *actually* produced.

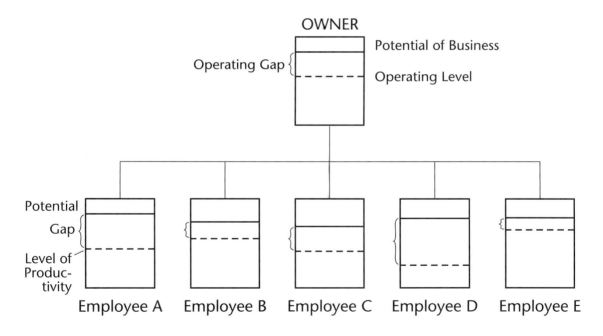

An *operational* gap—a gap between the true potential of your business to produce and the level at which it is currently operating—is also illustrated. An operational gap will always exist, regardless of how successful you are. Individuals and organizations can never consistently live up to their potential. As an owner, your challenge is to close the gaps of your employees, so that the organizational gap will be smaller. This will permit you to live up to your potential as the leader. How do you accomplish this goal?

You close the gaps of your employees by doing an excellent job in the field of human relations. You must, somehow, create healthy, warm relationships between yourself and your employees. You accomplish this when you follow the human relations principles and techniques presented in this book. Notice the difference between the previous diagram of a hypothetical small business and the one presented below.

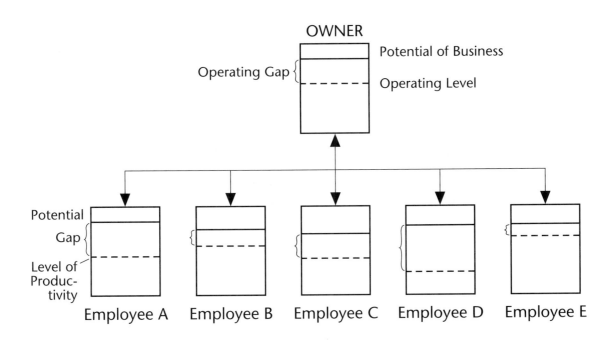

TWO-WAY COMMUNICATIONS

The only change is the addition of two-way arrows between you, the owner, and the five employees. What do these two-way arrows signify? They remind us that the primary way to build and maintain sound relationships is to have *two-way communication.* In other words, to increase productivity—close the operating gap—you must keep your employees informed, and be a good listener so they can communicate with you. The life blood of any relationship is two-way communications.

Following are other ideas that will help you close your operational gap:

Your first goal is to motivate your employees. You will need to inspire them to produce at their highest levels. Management books are full of motivational theories. Some, properly interpreted, can be useful. For example, from 1927 to 1932, the Western Electric Company conducted the "Hawthorne Experiments," which showed that *no matter what improvements* were made (e.g., rest periods, free hot lunches) the productivity of the team increased.

Why is this? *The employees were made to feel important.*

Until these experiments, management had accepted as self-evident that the way to improve the rate of production was to improve machinery, provide better lighting and make similar physical changes; the "Hawthorne Experiments" proved that the emotional climate of the worker is equally important.

PSYCHOLOGICAL NEEDS

What does this mean to you, as a beginning entrepreneur? Although you may not be able to provide all of the physical comforts for your *team,* you can help them feel a part of things, and satisfy their emotional needs more than larger firms usually accomplish.

One of the best known *need priority* lists was established by A. H. Maslow.* Maslow ranked needs as follows:

Maslow's Pyramid of Needs

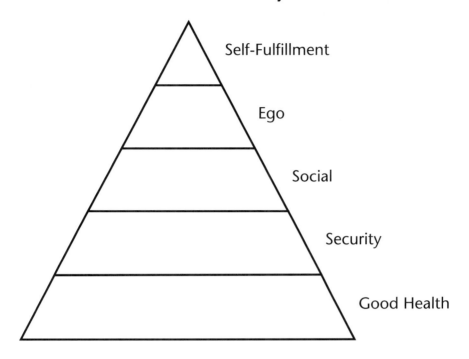

Self-Fulfillment

Ego

Social

Security

Good Health

The crux of this theory is that the bottom needs must be fulfilled before the others come into play. The bottom, base need is physiological—food, good health. Next is security and safety. Third from the bottom is social needs—one's need to be accepted and enjoy the company of others. Next are ego needs—recognition from others. Finally, at the pinnacle is one's need for self-fulfillment. As a small, beginning operator, you must do your best to satisfy your physical and security needs, and those of your team; then, go all out to satisfy the social, ego and self-fulfillment needs. As a small team with a clear goal—the success of your business—you have an edge over larger firms.

*A. H. Maslow, "A Theory of Human Motivation," *Psychological Review* 50 (1943), pp. 370–96.

You can satisfy the social needs of your team by allowing them to have some fun together. You can satisfy their *ego* needs by giving them opportunities to accomplish things they have never tried before—and praising them for their successes. You can, by making them full-fledged team members, give them the feeling of fulfillment, by enjoying any successes the new organization achieves.

Your Turn

List ten psychological needs of employees. Some management experts call these needs job satisfiers. *In making your list, take into consideration: (1) the needs you have in your present job, (2) the needs you have attempted to provide to employees in the past and (3) Maslow's pyramid of needs.*

Employee Needs

1.

2.

3.

4.

5.

6.

7.

8.

9.

10.

ADDITIONAL SUGGESTIONS

As you put into practice the employee needs—job satisfiers—you have just listed, keep the following suggestions in mind:

1. Building good relationships with team members is more important than being able to do the job skillfully yourself.

   The technical skills you have are important, because you must know how to do something before you can teach others; however, your emphasis as an owner will be on transmitting your skills through sound relationships, rather than doing the tasks yourself.

2. Spending time to restore or improve your relationship with a team member whose productivity has slipped is the most important thing you can do with your time.

   As an owner, in all likelihood you will have more things to do than time to do them in. It will be necessary to sift out and assign suitable priorities to your responsibilities. Always assign top priority to keeping the productivity of others as high as possible. Slipped productivity of one team member requires action on your part.

3. Expect to achieve high productivitiy in a hurry from new employees.

   Today, a faster pay-off is expected from new employees than was true in the past, because (1) employees have a shorter span of employment, (2) the pace inside most organizations—including yours—is faster and (3) training is more expensive.

4. The future of your business will be based upon the productivity of the people who now work for you.

   All of the ideas presented in this book are designed to help you form a *team* of workers who will produce more than those in competitive jobs. This, in turn, will give you the edge you need to succeed.

ASK YOURSELF

▶ Why is building good working relationships with employees more important than the non-management tasks you perform yourself?

▶ Explain the phenomenon that some employees with modest potential out-produce their co-workers with higher potential.

▶ What would you do if you discovered you had hired a part-time employee with a modest potential who, after completing his or her trial period, despite repeated training, was unable to meet your productivity standards?

CHAPTER
EIGHT

PEAK

AND

DOWN

PERIODS

STAFFING AND EMPLOYEE ATTITUDE CONSIDER-ATIONS

When it comes to sales, few new business operations move up month after month at a regular pace. Most have peak and down periods. This is especially true of retail operations, but manufacturing shops, businesses connected with the seasons, and even real estate agencies fluctuate.

Peak and down periods present two basic problems. One is staffing considerations. It normally takes a large staff to handle peak periods effectively, but during slow periods fewer people are needed. The second problem involves employee attitudes. Idle workers usually become more negative than busy employees.

What about your type of business? Will you discover that there are ups and downs in sales that present special kinds of problems? If so, this chapter is designed to help you have better control over your personnel during the high and low sales periods.

Noriko opened her combination book/gift store on the first of October, in time to capitalize on the Christmas season. Noriko got off to a good start due to an excellent opening promotion in October, early Christmas buying in November, and rewarding sales in December. Then came a bleak January and a worse February. Although March was a turnaround month, it was a slow spring and summer. Sales did not get back on track until September.

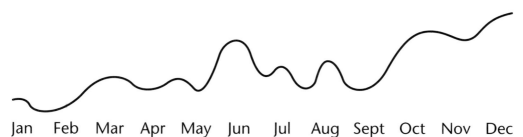

Jan   Feb   Mar   Apr   May   Jun   Jul   Aug   Sept   Oct   Nov   Dec

STAFFING FOR PEAK AND SLOW PERIODS

The big advantage in having part-time help is that you can adjust your staff easily to peak and low activity periods. Many small retailers quickly learn the advantages of having one or more *on call* employees. An *on call* employee is usually willing to drop what they are doing and report for work after receiving a telephone call. College students and housewives who do not have small children are the best prospects for *on call* status.

EXAMPLE

Maria operates a successful ice cream and cookie store with one full-time assistant manager, three regular part-timers, and an on call list that usually includes a dozen possibilities. The best on call employees are at the top of the list. When one of her regular part-timers is ill, Maria or her manager get on the telephone and go down the list. Although there may be a wait of thirty minutes to an hour for the employee to get to work, they are seldom under or over staffed.

Even with the best personnel planning, it is not easy for a small operator to keep employees sufficiently busy during slow periods, to keep their attitudes positive. What do most retailers do? *They keep an assignment list.*

EXAMPLE

Kwan operates a franchise auto-parts store in a small town. He realized that there would be days when customers would be few. He installed a small blackboard in the back of the store with a sign on the top that reads: CUSTOMERS COME FIRST BUT KEEP BUSY WITH THESE ASSIGNMENTS IN BETWEEN. On the blackboard, Kwan keeps a running list of assignments that include everything from washing windows and changing displays, to calling clients whose special orders have arrived. Kwan checks to see if assignments are carried out and changes his list each day.

Many small business owners try to provide a minimum of four hours of work to both part-time and on-call employees, to make their efforts—getting ready for work, commuting, etc.—worthwhile. Of course, when there is a large supply of available part-timers, it may be possible to drop that minimum as low as two hours per period of work. To those who live nearby, two hours of work may be better than nothing, or may fit into their schedules better than longer periods. In discussing the problem with one owner, she said, "Last Saturday, business was great and I needed more workers. Today is the opposite. Even so, I bite the bullet and try to provide them with a four hour shift. Keeping a staff just the right size is a real challenge."

ATTITUDE AND INACTIVITY

Workers who do not have idle time on the job are almost always more positive and upbeat than those who do not have enough to do. Most small business operators accept the premise that busy employees are happy and productive employees. On the other hand, workers who are permitted to have idle time turn negative and their productivity drops.

EXAMPLE

Vadim opened up a mail box franchise in a new neighborhood shopping center last year. He started with one part-timer. As sales increased, he needed two people to assist customers. Soon, Vadim noticed that his salespeople were often standing around waiting for customers. This did not bother him until he discovered that the waiting around caused his salespeople to become negative. When a customer did enter the store, his salespeople were not prepared psychologically to serve the individual. What did Vadim learn from his insightful conclusion? Always keep your help busy.

Although each operation has special peak and slow period problems, surveys show that customers in retail stores are generally happier with the treatment they receive during peak periods. No one has been able to identify exactly why. Is it because employees like to be busy, and they have better attitudes when they have more customers to serve? Or is it because customers are patient when they notice how busy the salespeople are? It is probably some of both. Most people recognize that standing around waiting for something to do on the job causes negative drift in one's attitude. Time moves slowly. One's mind strays away from work. Slowly, without knowing it, attitudes deteriorate. *This often happens even when there is plenty of non-customer work to be done.*

The solution lies in management planning. When customer activity is low, backup jobs should receive priority. They should be made as exciting as possible. While doing these tasks, employees need to be trained to keep an eye out for customers. No matter what else needs to be accomplished, the customer always comes first. As we have said repeatedly, your primary advantage in a small business is *the personal service you can provide.*

Your Turn

Assume that you operate a business that has peak **and** slow **customer activity, and that you accept the principle that an idle employee is usually a negative one.**

- ► How would you keep your staff busy at all times?

- ► Would you use a variation of the *blackboard* idea?

- ► If so, how would you make it work for you?

- ► What role would part-timers or *on call* employees play? Outline your plan below:

ADDITIONAL SUGGESTIONS

Listed below are some additional suggestions that might assist you in adjusting to the ups and downs of your business.

SUGGESTION 1: Take the long view

When you did your original planning for your operation, you made projections of sales figures, gross profit and net profit you hoped to achieve. You may have been encouraged to have a three-year plan, so that you would not worry so much about month-to-month figures. *But it is only natural for a small business owner to set out monthly figures.* The problem comes when owners start to sweat out *daily* or *weekly* sales figures. Pretty soon, their attitudes are bouncing around like a yo-yo. On a good day, their attitudes are up; on a slow day, they are down. For control and planning purposes, a monthly analysis is essential, but it is the first annual report that has significance. And, as you look ahead, keep in mind that many businesses are not successful until after three years of operation.

EXAMPLE

When Anita opened her fashion boutique, she was riding on cloud nine. After a full year of operation, she wanted to talk to her landlord about breaking her lease. Then, a combination of three things gave Anita courage. First, she cut down her overhead to the point that she and two part-timers did all the work themselves. Second, she became a more astute buyer. Third, she started to build a clientele that she could buy for. As a result, with the exception of January and February she broke even her second year. Finally, before her third year was over, Anita was paying herself a good salary and the business was showing a 10 percent net profit on sales volume. Looking back, Anita made this statement: "I can't tell you the number of times I was willing to give up. And, during these down periods, I was my own worst enemy, because my own attitude was defeating me. It is a mistake to start any business if you are not willing to sweat out some tough times. I owe a lot to my husband and my banker for keeping me going."

SUGGESTION 2: Chart your peak and low periods

It takes a few months of operation before you can do this and, at best, it is only a projection. It is worth doing for two reasons: one, you cannot make the best use of part-timers without knowing when they are needed. Two, you want to be on board yourself when activity is at its highest. Keep in mind that research indicates customers are more tolerant and easier to serve when a place is busy. In other words, the best time to *make it* is during peak periods. Build up your peak periods. Train yourself and your staff to take advantage of slow periods, to build better relationships with customers.

SUGGESTION 3: All of your efforts may fall short of your goal if you do not keep your *own* attitude up

Keep in mind that your employees have little radar sets that are tuned in to *your* attitude. When you are positive, it is much easier for them to be upbeat. When you are *down* they are more apt to follow your lead. As a small business owner, it is a good idea to share good news with your staff, but do not *unload* your problems on them. If they suspect your business is in trouble, they may start looking elsewhere.

SUGGESTION 4: Train a replacement for yourself

One of the big advantages of a *mom-and-pop* operation is that when one spouse is not available, the other is prepared to take over alone, at least for a short period of time. In cases in which a business is a one-person operation—no spouse or one who is not interested—a replacement for the owner needs to be trained. As one shopowner explained:

> *"I guess I must have worked myself too hard and too many hours during the preparation and opening periods of my shop. At any rate, three months after the opening I was in the hospital. The good news during my two-week absence was Evita. She was my full-time employee and I had trained her to take over if I couldn't be there. She did a marvelous job. I've made a lot of mistakes since I started this place, but hiring and training Evita wasn't one of them. If this operation succeeds and I go for a second location, Evita will be in charge."*

Training your replacement should start before you are open for business. You may find it necessary to be absent to attend service club meetings, make buying trips, because of illness or family responsibility. Even if you are away for only a few hours, you want a capable and trustworthy manager to take over.

Here are three tips that may assist you in achieving this goal:

▶ Keep this need in mind during your initial interviews. Try to find a back-up person whom you feel you can trust and would follow your policies.

▶ Teach this person to do everything you do, with the exception of making major decisions. Share much of your financial data and other *inside* information necessary to make your operation successful.

▶ Make sure that other employees know this person is your assistant and in full command of the business in your absence.

Finally, see that your assistant understands how to utilize part-timers, to make the most of peak periods and keep labor costs at a minimum during periods of low activity.

EXAMPLE

When Hank started his small business, he had every confidence that he would be able to pay the rent, personnel and other overhead costs until the operation reached the break-even point. Six months into the business, Hank discovered he could not pull it off. Hank decided that the only solution was to go back to his old job. His previous employer had said Hank could return at any time. During the day, when Hank was on his old job, he had the person he had trained to take over run things. Hank took over on week-ends and they met each evening during the week to make decisions. How did it turn out? Hank held his old job until the business showed a small monthly profit.

ASK YOURSELF

▶ If you accept the *keep busy positive attitude* idea that supports the premise that idle workers become negative and both productivity and customer relationships suffer, what do you indend to do to keep employees energized during periods of low activity?

▶ If you plan to chart and analyze the peak and down periods that develop in your business, and accept the challenge of utilizing part-timers to help you make the most of both periods, describe your plan to do this.

▶ Do you accept the responsibility of developing a replacement for yourself? Discuss your plan to find, designate and train another employee, or to work as a team with your spouse.

CHAPTER NINE

HOW TO GET HIGHER PRODUCTIVITY FROM PART-TIMERS

LOWER PERSONNEL COSTS AND INCREASE PRODUCTIVITY

According to government census figures, almost 20 percent of the current workforce is made up of part-time employees. It is estimated this percentage will climb to 30 percent or more before the turn of the century. The majority of these part-timers will be recruited and managed by small business organizations. The question becomes: *How can you lower personnel costs and increase productivity through the efficient use of part-timers?*

Three steps are involved. *Step one* is to evaluate how many jobs can or should be part-time, as opposed to full-time. *Step two* is how to recruit the best available part-timers. *Step three* is to work with part-timers, so that they will be high producers and full members of the team.

This chapter explains how to work with part-timers, especially the young, unsettled employee who may still be in high school or college, or finds it impossible to locate and win a full-time position. Chapter 10 discusses how many, within your total employee mix, should be part-timers.

TEN TIPS ON HOW TO ACHIEVE HIGH PRODUCTIVITY FROM YOUNG PART-TIMERS

1. ***Follow the principle that learning can be its own reward.*** Young, qualified, inexperienced individuals can make a major contribution to the productivity of almost any organization—and, they can do this at minimum or near-minimum wages. How can you accomplish this? Tell them in advance that you will compensate for their lower early remuneration by giving them learning experiences that will prepare them for future salary advances.

EXAMPLE

Tony and Gabriella operate their Spaghetti House #1 with 90 percent part-time help. They have only three full-time employees on the payroll. How do they attract such capable part-timers when they pay only slightly above the minimum wage standards? They provide such excellent training that their part-timers know they are preparing for better jobs elsewhere.

Joan, a part-time college student, puts it this way: "Even with tips, which we split with part-timers behind the scenes, I make only $7 per hour. But I am learning how to improve my personality by dealing with adults under high-tempo conditions. In one way, you could say that I receive two paychecks."

2. ***Give young workers more responsibility than they are used to receiving.*** Most students or recent graduates can handle more work responsibility than they have been given in the past. All that most of them want is an opportunity to demonstrate they are ready.

EXAMPLE

When Avani gave Nichole a chance to serve clients on the second day she was on the job, her husband, Nayan, was skeptical. By the end of the day, Nayan complimented both Avani and Nichole. Although she was just sixteen and had another year until she would finish high school, Nicole acted in a mature and professional manner. Customers liked her from the start. The confidence Avani showed in her was all that was needed.

3. ***Use compliments to build up the image young employees have of themselves.*** It is one thing to get high grades at school; it is something else to produce satisfactory results as a worker. Most adults remember their first job and paycheck vividly; they remember even more the individual and business where they enjoyed their first success as a worker.

EXAMPLE

When Kenji got his first summer job, working in a service station, he was fearful that his immaturity would work against him. By the end of the summer, his boss and the mechanics hated to see him return to school. Kenji had become a part of the team. In record time, through hard work, a willingness to accept all assignments, and a great attitude toward customers, he had learned how to work with adults. Without knowing it, the full-time workers had given Kenji a new self-image that would help him throughout his life.

4. ***Adopt the "give me your best while you are here" policy.*** Although many adults occupy and prefer permanent part-time jobs, most young people consider themselves temporary workers. Many work after school or

college, during vacation periods, or knowing that they will eventually move on to another position. Those employers who make the best use of young part-timers accept this temporary status, and ask only that the employees give their best as long as they are on the payroll. Most employers *want* their part-timers to move on when they have qualified for something better. In fact, they frequently take some credit for helping the employees prepare for such a move.

EXAMPLE

Jeremy worked in Ysabel's branch bank for four years as a part-timer—twenty hours per-week while he was in college, and extra hours during vacation periods. During this period, Jeremy learned the banking business and occupied all positions on a temporary basis. Upon graduation as a chemist, he was given a farewell party that clearly showed he was respected for giving his best for the entire period.

5. ***Provide some room for laughter and a little horse-play.*** No matter how much responsibility young people assume, or how high their productivity may be, they like to have a little fun when it is appropriate. Small business owners who accept and go along with this premise not only get higher performance from their part-timers, they also attract other capable people to take their place when they leave.

EXAMPLE

Genevieve operates an old-fashioned ice cream store. During the summer months, things get hectic. She is fully dependent upon young part-timers. Although she expects and receives high performance all day long, when the store closes at night everyone is encouraged to relax and have a little fun. Birthdays are celebrated with special ice cream cakes; everyone is encouraged to prepare a special dessert—as long as they eat it—and they all enjoy it for a half-hour, with pay.

What two suggestions from your own experiences will help you achieve higher productivity from younger part-timers?

6. ***Provide a reasonable, consistent discipline line and see that it is honored.*** Most young people are willing to follow a few simple rules, as long as they understand them, that everyone is treated the same, and that they have some freedom to enjoy their work. What they do not like is working for an owner who is inconsistent, *picky* and inflexible.

EXAMPLE

Vu and Kim opened their mail order business three years ago, with one full-time and seven part-timers. Vu, the strong member of the family, decided that it was not necessary to establish a discipline line—that is, set up a few rules regarding absenteeism, taking breaks, and the type of behavior expected. As a result, the work environment was so permissive that it was impossible to develop a cohesive team. Vu later reversed her position and established a discipline line that was overbearing and did not provide enough freedom. Today, after further adjustments, Vu and Kim have a discipline line that everyone fully understands and respects. Had Vu and Kim started out with a carefully thought-out list of simple rules, they would have saved themselves many problems and enhanced their success.

7. ***Accept mistakes without converting them into major issues.*** Everyone, regardless of age, makes mistakes. Young, inexperienced workers can be expected to make a few more. When mistakes are downplayed instead of highlighted, people learn faster and make fewer mistakes in the future. A pat on the back with the comment "you'll get the hang of it before you know it," will go a lot further in building a strong, productive employee than a *chew out* session. As irritating as the mistakes your employees make may be, try to handle them with finesse and, when appropriate, a sense of humor.

EXAMPLE

On the second day that Jill was being trained as a waitress, she dropped a tray of glasses during the peak of the dinner trade. Embarrassed, she was ready to quit if she was not terminated. What did happen? The owner helped Jill clean up the mess and gave her a few moments to gain her composure. Later, when things were slower, he told Jill that her initiation was over and that she had joined the team. Jill became one of the most productive part-timers on the staff.

8. ***Train part-timers to be team members, as though they were full-timers.*** It is vital to the success of any business that part-timers be fully integrated into the *team* along with full-timers, temps and other workstyles. Part-timers who are left on the outside looking in seldom reach their productivity potential.

EXAMPLE

Joyce was employed as a part-timer to help reduce the work load of Clara, who was in charge of the copying section of a large insurance firm. From the first day, Joyce was treated the same as a full-timer. She was invited to attend staff meetings, involved in solving problems and given all possible considerations. As a result, Joyce's hourly production soon reached, and then passed, that of the full-time people. While Clara was away on her annual vacation, Joyce demonstrated her skills by taking over, on a full-time basis. When Clara returned, Joyce was promoted into a full-time role and another part-timer was hired to take her place.

9. ***Promising part-timers that if they do a good job they will become full-timers is seldom a wise move.*** A promise is usually interpreted by the part-timer as a firm commitment. To promise a part-timer such a reward is often premature, decreases motivation and often turns the part-timer negative; he or she *waits* to be promoted instead of concentrating on preparing for the possibility of a promotion. If they desire full-time roles, part-timers know without being told that they are on probation. They recognize that their job is a kind of internship that may, when productivity reaches a high level, be converted into a full-time position.

EXAMPLE

When Gregg graduated from college, the only job he could find was an internship role with a marketing firm. He was told that full-time employees were usually selected from interns, but not always. No promises were made.

Within six weeks, Gregg knew this was the company for him. He immediately set out to make a bigger contribution than the other three interns. Although he worked only the prescribed twenty hours per week, he earned his way into a full team membership role. After one year as a part-timer, two of his three competitors had resigned. Gregg was chosen over the third for a full-time position. Although some of his friends thought it was foolish for him to pay such a price, Gregg knew what he wanted and soon discovered that his new job was worth working and waiting for.

10. ***Provide individual training and counseling to fit the needs of the part-timer.*** It is easy to neglect young part-timers, once they get adjusted and reach normal productivity levels. This can be a mistake, because they need the support of a *mentor* to guide them in the right direction, more than full-time employees. Part-timers want to know how they are doing. Should they go back to school for skill training? What books should they read for self-improvement?

When Mira first brought part-timers into her department, she neglected to give them formal appraisal interviews, which she was required to do with full-timers. Mira agreed when a part-timer asked to be included in the program. She discovered it was so beneficial that she extended the process to all part-timers. The appraisals resulted in a measurable increase of productivity in her department.

Your Turn   **List the tips covered in this chapter that would apply to adult part-timers, retirees and full-time employees—that is, which tips would increase productivity of any employee?**

ASK YOURSELF

► What about your attitude will help you gain higher productivity from young part-timers? Would you enjoy working with them? Can you build your new business around part-timers?

► Are you a supporter of the "give me your best while you are here" policy? Why or why not?

► Discuss the concept that many small business owners can get higher per hour productivity from a few part-timers than full-timers, and can save labor costs by doing it.

CHAPTER TEN

ACHIEVING THE RIGHT EMPLOYEE MIX

THE BASIC GOAL

Ask yourself this question: "When it comes to creating my staff, what should my basic goals be?" First, to get the highest possible productivity from each member. Next, to keep costs down with the best mix of full and part-time employees. Third, to do this while you build a compatible *team* that will stay with you, and will grow into better jobs as your business permits. On top of these goals, you will want to employ a mix of employees that will reflect the cultural diversity of your community.

Most small business operators start out with only a few employees. One or two might be full-time employees who receive comprehensive benefits. The rest may be less than full-time and receive only those benefits required by law. In many cases, this includes only Social Security and Workman's Compensation. The idea is to design the right *mix* for your type of business. It is always best to start with a bare minimum and add employees as the business demands. Mama and Papa operations often start out with no additional employees. The first person on the payroll may be a part-timer.

SMALL BUSINESS OPERATIONS THRIVE ON PART-TIMERS

Federal legislation defines a part-timer as a person who works less than 1,000 hours per year ($17\frac{1}{2}$ hours per week) for the same firm. It is generally accepted, however, that a part-timer is an employee who works fewer than thirty hours per week. The average is closer to twenty. Policing the number of hours a part-timer works in a year is obviously difficult, because of seasonal needs and the high turnover of such employees.

Part-timers are divided into two basic groups—those who prefer to work part-time for their own reasons, and those who cannot find regular, full-time employment.

Normally, those who prefer part-time work have a primary focus other than employment. A good example is a college student taking a full load of courses. Another example is a mother or father with children, who does not wish to be away from home for extended periods.

Those unable to find full-time employment usually seek and hold part-time jobs on a short-term basis, hoping that their part-time roles might expand into full-time career positions, or that they can find full-time positions elsewhere.

Part-time jobs usually, but not always, have these characteristics:

- ▶ Wages are typically low.

- ▶ Only the basic or required benefits (Social Security & Workers' Compensation) are usually provided.

- ▶ There is usually less job security for part-time job holders.

Many part-time positions are long-term. A few are designed to attract and keep workers with specific skills. For example, it is not unusual to find a waitress in a restaurant who has been on a twenty-hour week for over twenty years.

Some service firms—retail stores, restaurants, banks, etc.—operate profitably because the vast majority of their personnel are part-timers. Some are used only during *peak* periods, when the business is serving more customers. Thus, part-time employees give many types of businesses high productivity, flexibility and lower labor costs.

Generally speaking, the more a start-up business can operate at a high level, with only part-time employees, the better. Not only are part-time hourly rates lower, but fewer benefits are required. Benefits for full-time employees often reach 40 percent of the individual's salary. Thus, a full-time employee being paid a salary equivalent to $10 per hour would make $400 per week, plus $160 in benefits, or $560. On the other hand, a part-time employee, working at $5 per hour for twenty hours plus minimum benefits, would earn close to $115. The cost of two twenty-hour part-timers would approximate $230, which would be less than one-half a regular, full-time employee.

Small wonder that it is estimated that over 70 percent of small business employees work on a part-time basis.

In addition to part-timers, it is often less expensive for small operators to employee free lancers (e.g., a CPA for accounting and tax purposes), *temps* on a full-time basis for a short time (peak periods), and WAHs (work-at-home people) who can contribute to productivity, without needing office or other space.

After one year of operation, a typical scenario for a Mama and Papa Graphics Shop might be:

- ▶ Both husband and wife work extended hours

- ▶ One full-time forty hours per week employee

- ▶ Three part-timers

- ▶ Two free lancers—one a CPA and tax specialist, the other an artist who works at home.

The basic idea is to develop the best possible mix of workstyles for best results. This takes advanced thinking and planning. For example, the employment of a full-time employee is a major commitment. If such an individual makes it through a probationary period, termination can become most complicated, as certain laws must be honored. In most cases, an entrepreneur starting out should refrain from employing a full-time person unless the business demands it, or if part-timers who can be trained are unavailable.

Small Business Owners Usually Hire Their Own Part-Timers

If a temp is employed for a short time on a full-time basis, she or he is not a part-timer. However, if a temp is employed on a part-time basis for either a short or lengthy period, it would be natural for the temp agency and the firm to refer to the individual as a part-timer. Other ways to distinguish a temp from a typical part-timer include:

- ▶ A temp usually works through an agency. The agency recruits, interviews and hires workers, and then places them with organizations *at a profit.*

▶ In most cases, the agency takes care of Social Security and Worker's Compensation, and may provide additional benefits.

▶ The employing organization pays the temp agency, who, in-turn, pays the employee.

▶ Temps often work full-time for short periods in one organization and then, through the help of the agency, move on to a new firm.

▶ When a temp employee is unsatisfactory, the employer contacts the agency who is responsible for the behavior of the worker.

Organizations are most interested in the employment of temps when they have an immediate, but temporary, need for one or more full-timers with specific skills. Under these conditions, it is profitable to employ temps and transfer the problem of recruiting and processing to an outside agency. Organizations who have seasonal *highs* often bring in temps to assist them during peak periods.

Although most temp agencies specialize in furnishing skilled office employees, they are currently moving into all skill areas.

People looking for work often prefer working through *temp* agencies because they (1) can work more flexible hours, (2) gain training and experience in many environments in a hurry, (3) may find a company they really like and eventually qualify for full-time positions and (4) once assignments are completed, they can take a break before beginning the next.

The term *contingent worker* is used frequently these days to signify any individual who does not work a full, forty hours per week, with comprehensive benefits. Part-timers, temps, free-lancers, contract-employees and consultants fall under this *contingency* umbrella.

Advantages of Employing Part-timers

Advantages listed apply to all part-timers, and they are more true of younger, high school and college age employees.

1. Costs are significantly lower on an hour per hour basis. Some part-timers are paid less than half of what full-timers who do the same work are paid. Many small businesses would be forced to close without part-timers.

2. Generally speaking, part-timers are more energetic and enthusiastic. They sometimes *liven up* the workplace; full-timers pick up their work tempos as well.

3. When full-time positions open up, employers can make better choices from part-timers, whom they have had the opportunity to observe and test out.

4. Young part-timers often have better learning attitudes.

5. Many part-timers prefer to work peak periods and are willing to be available on an *on call* basis.

6. Most part-timers are willing to accept and do well with routine and unpleasant assignments.

7. The less sophisticated the jobs, the better part-timers perform, permitting full-timers to devote their time to more difficult assignments.

8. Part-timers are often more appreciative and easier to work with than full-timers.

9. Some smaller and isolated communities offer a larger supply of responsible and hard-working part-timers, because fewer part-time jobs are available.

10. Add an advantage of your own:

   _____

   _____

   _____

Disadvantages of Employing Part-timers

1. Part-timers are less committed to their jobs; they usually have a long-term goal that is more important. This causes them to be less stable and dependable. For example, you might train an outstanding performer to assume a more responsible assignment and then have the individual leave. Even with careful recruitment, turnover among part-timers can be very high compared with full-timers.

2. Absenteeism is generally higher among part-timers.

3. In contrast to experienced and retired part-timers, younger applicants are less professional, because of their lack of experience.

4. Young part-timers require more training.

5. They are more apt to make costly mistakes.

6. Generally speaking, part-timers require a more tolerant, patient and understanding attitude from employers.

7. It is often more difficult to select the best available part-timers, because they have less experience behind them. Some employers claim that they have more success with younger part-timers who have good grade point averages.

8. Younger part-timers often socialize more on the job than full-timers do.

9. Some employers claim that part-timers have less follow-through on the job and, as a result, do not do well on responsible assignments.

10. Add a disadvantage of your own:

    _____

    _____

    _____

Qualified Part-timers Are Highly Available in Most Communities

The reservoir of applicants seeking full or part-time jobs has risen drastically. This is due, in large measure, to increases in women entering the workforce and in the number of organizations that have down-sized their personnel. It is anticipated that the availability of those who will accept part-time work will remain high into the next century. Following are some reasons why:

▶ Traditional, 40-hour week, full-benefit positions will continue to shrink as organizations continue to down-size, to cut overhead expenses.

▶ The pool of available students will remain high as they compete for the best part-time jobs to help cover increasing educational costs. In some cases, graduates, unable to find full-time positions, will hold down two or more part-time jobs.

▶ Retirees are actively seeking more part-time involvements at the present time. This trend will continue, if inflation grows and/or retirement pensions shrink.

▶ More parents are choosing to spend additional time at home with their children, even if it means seeking part-time jobs. Young couples have figured out that with one spouse working full-time—with benefits that cover the entire family—the other can work part-time, on a flex-schedule that permits extra time at home.

▶ Moonlighting will continue. Even when employment is high, full-time workers who want more money will seek *after work* part-time positions.

Part-timers Can Be Substitutes for Full-timers

When we think of part-time employees, we usually think of food servers, delivery couriers who work after school, office workers who do specific jobs for two or four hours, three or four days a week, or people hired to perform limited functions, who may or may not require supervision.

This is the thinking of the past.

Today, part-timers are an integral part of the workforce. We must accept more flexible scheduling. We must recognize that employees can produce the same results, in short or split shifts, as full-time workers produce in a normal forty hour work week. Consider the following:

- ► Imagine a part-time employee becoming a contributing member of your work team, even if she or he is present only fifteen hours a week.

- ► Think about a production line that operates with only part-timers, three days per week.

- ► Visualize yourself, or a friend who needs the income, holding down two or three part-time jobs until you qualify for a full-time position with full benefits.

- ► Picture two people sharing the same job on different shifts, and producing much more than a single employee.

The era of the full-time employee with full benefits is under fire because of the escalating cost to employers of health care and other benefits. Also, the traditional eight-hour shift often produces only six hours of productivity. Two part-timers, working four hours, might produce more, at a substantially lower cost. Thus, as long as there is a labor pool and people who want to work, part-timers will be in demand.

FREE LANCERS, CONSULTANTS AND INDIVIDUALS WHO WORK IN THEIR HOMES

Some small business owners can profitably utilize free lancers, consultants and individuals who work in their homes (WAHs). For example, entrepreneurs often go to free-lance artists to design their logos, advertising brochures and other graphic presentations.

Although large corporations more frequently use outside consultants, small business operators can go to financial experts, marketing specialists and others for assistance, and pay a fee for such services. More often, however, the beginning entrepreneur will seek free advice from his or her banker, family advisors or friends who operate successful businesses. Of course, most small operators maintain a close relationship with a CPA or lawyer for professional advice on a regular basis. These professionals are not generally classified as consultants.

Many large and small businesses have employees who work in their homes. It is a growing workstyle, and under certain circumstances has advantages for both parties.

Your Turn

This three-year Workstyle Mix Schedule *is a tool to help you plan the best mix for your business during your first three years of operation. In the left-hand column, you will find six workstyles popular among small business operators. For each year, in each category, write the number of persons you plan to employ as your business expands.*

Workstyle Mix Schedule

	Year One	*Year Two*	*Year Three*
Full-time employees with comprehensive benefits			
Part-time employees with minimum benefits			
Free-lance or outside consultants—professionals such as artists, lawyers, CPAs			
Temps—full-time employees hired through an agency to help during peak periods— the *temp* agency pays the benefits			
Part or full-time employees who work for you out of their homes			

In this chapter you will consider the variety of workstyles that you can form into your successful team. As you do this, keep the following in mind:

PROBATIONARY PERIODS ARE ESSENTIAL

A two-week or thirty-day probationary or *trial* period is recommended for all new employees. This gives both parties a chance to size up the situation. The employee can test the work environment, skills required and future possibilities. The employer can test how the new person will produce and fit into the *team*. Up to the day the trial period is over, either party can cancel the arrangement.

Long-term Personnel Factors

In building the personnel of a small business, give careful consideration to the following factors:

Quality As Well As High Productivity—In your desire to achieve high productivity—the name of the game—it is easy to sacrifice quality. If this happens, you can permanently injure the reputation—image—of your small business.

EXAMPLE

After the first six months of operation, Polly's Pies was a growing concern. Business had nearly doubled every month. When Polly's CPA told her that she needed to double her net profit, she made the mistake of buying supplies from a less expensive resource. In the process, the quality of her pies deteriorated slightly and her sales flattened out. Polly should have lowered her overhead expenses, not the quality of her pie ingredients.

There is no substitute for quality when building a small business of any kind. The product or service you provide—or both—must be superior to that of your competition. Being equal is not good enough.

Lower Cost Per Unit—Although overhead costs can be reduced using a variety of methods, the greatest savings must come from personnel costs. This is why your *workstyle mix* is so significant. You need to keep your labor cost at a minimum—under your competitors'—while you keep your quality higher.

When Tomas opened his Cycle Shop, he was the only employee for three months—preferring to work sixty hours a week before putting anyone on the staff. His first employee was a bicycle enthusiast who wanted to work only twenty hours a week. She turned out to be outstanding with customers. Tomas paid her just above the minimum wage. Since she wanted to learn how to repair her own bike and those of her family, he compensated by teaching her how to do minor repairs.

At the end of three years, the Cycle Shop had seven part-time employees—all learning to do repairs under close guidance—and one free lancer, a CPA. As a result of his low overhead, Thomas was able to do quality work at prices slightly below those of his larger competitors. The volume of traffic enabled him to sell more new bicycles and related equipment.

Part-time employees who are given the opportunity to learn and experience personal growth are often high producers and loyal employees. True, they may move on to permanent jobs with higher benefits, but they make a major contribution while they are your employees.

Fewer Human Relations Problems—If you were to interview small business operators in your community, you would discover that, in most cases, their number one problem comes from their employees. Employee problems spring from poor hiring procedures, poor training, over-promising and the failure of the entrepreneur to listen to and counsel employees.

A few learn the secret of keeping labor costs down without generating such problems. These are employers, like Thomas, who help their employees grow. They stick with their best workstyle mix, see that each employee feels a part of the *team* and is prepared for the future. In other words, the owner builds mutually rewarding relationships with all employees, without unnecessarily increasing labor costs.

▶ Each small business is different, so you cannot always look to others for your best mix.

▶ College students can be outstanding learners and producers.

▶ Adults who wish to work part-time so they can spend more time with their children can be outstanding producers.

▶ Retirees are frequently excellent part-time employees.

▶ Full-time employees who turn sour after passing probationary periods can be serious problems.

▶ In defining your best workstyle mix, take your own personality and willingness to train new employees into consideration.

▶ Be aware that it is easy to double your troubles should you bring in a family member who expects a special workstyle that is not in harmony with the *team* spirit of others.

For more on this subject, see *Managing the Family Business* by Marshall Northington, Crisp Publications, 1993.

ASK YOURSELF

▶ Describe your preference for a two-week or thirty-day trial period for all new employees.

▶ Due to costs involved, discuss your news on the employment of a minimum of full-timers and a maximum of part-timers.

▶ In your type of business, how possible is it to get higher hour-by-hour productivity from a part-timer than a full-timer?

CHAPTER
ELEVEN

COMMON

HUMAN

MISTAKES

RECOGNIZE YOUR OWN WEAK- NESSES

Danger! Beware! You are about to read about people mistakes that can cause a small business to fail *even though all other factors spell success.* Many highly capable entrepreneurs have discovered, too late, that they have fallen into a serious trap. The primary cause for making such human errors is failure to recognize one's own weaknesses ahead of time. This chapter describes common practices you will want to avoid. In all instances, these mistakes will destroy healthy, open, productive relationships between you and your staff.

1. ***Having two bosses.*** Starting a small business from scratch should be a one-leader operation. This does not mean a mom-and-pop arrangement is doomed from the start, but it does mean that, as far as other employees are concerned, there should be one leader of the team. Although a husband-wife combination may split duties and responsibilities, only one person should be in charge of personnel. One person out of the partnership should give employees directions, do counseling and so forth. When one person is away, the other is a substitute. Naturally, the owner who is best with people and *likes* to work with people should be selected, while the other person might be responsible for the financial and operational sides of the business.

2. ***Being over-familiar with employees.*** In operating a small business, the "we are a family" concept can be taken too far. Just as in larger organizations, relationships should be built on a *business* basis. Misunderstandings can occur when relationships are allowed to become highly personal.

   Employees may misinterpret what owners say; owners may take advantage of employees. All of the laws dealing with discrimination and sexual harassment apply as much to the small business as to the large corporation. Ethical behavior on the part of owners is mandatory.

   Face it. Starting a new business brings people close together. It is easy to turn what should be a pure working relationship into something highly personal. This places the owner in a vulnerable position, should the other party become disenchanted later.

Although discrimination is most apt to occur during the employment process, employees must be treated fairly in every respect once they are on the payroll—no racial prejudice, no sexual discrimination, no age preference. Today, employees have easy legal recourse when they feel they have been discriminated against on the job. Small business operations, just getting up a full head of steam, do not need to be slowed down with discrimination suits.

3. ***Making too many promises and not keeping those made.*** When starting a new business and you have one or more employees who really dig in and produce above others, it is natural to promise them favors should things turn out well in the future. Such promises often lead to misunderstandings and conflicts. It is much better to compliment high producers as you go, than to make promises you may not be able to fulfill. Keep in mind that a promise is an emotional commitment. Employees do not forget them.

Your Turn   ***List three human relations mistakes,*** not *covered so far, that you sense you are exceptionally vulnerable to and, as a result, you could make unconsciously. In other words, list mistakes you might make because you know yourself well enough to know they* could *happen. Once listed and recognized, your chances of making the mistakes will be reduced.*

4. ***Playing favorites.*** The easy way to irritate regular employees is to hire a family member and give this person special treatment. Many owners who hire their own children expect more from them than regular employees. Some go too far in the other direction. This does not mean that an owner should not employ family members—one of the advantages of owning your own business. It means that you should raise the caution flag when you make such decisions. Nepotism—having family members employed in the same organization—is not illegal, but it needs to be handled sensitively, so that non-family members are not turned away. When both the owner and the family employee see the picture clearly, it can be a positive move; everybody loses when the opposite occurs.

   The basic principle involved is to always treat people equally and fairly, in an open, honorable manner. That is why a few basic personnel rules, openly stated, make as much sense in a small business as in a large one.

5. ***Hiring new employees on a hunch.*** It is easy to be over-casual in hiring new workers. The results are far better when you have the applicant fill out a standard form, you check on at least one reference, and you make an objective decision, based upon *all* available applicants. Keep in mind the procedures recommended in Chapter 3. Professional interviewers sometimes make hiring mistakes; the small owner pays a higher price for mistakes.

6. ***Failure to set high standards.*** Although making a long list of standards that cannot be monitored is probably a poor use of time, having a few personnel standards in writing is recommended. Most sizable firms have *Personnel Handbooks* that outline rules, procedures and standards. Small business operators should create *mini versions* and make certain that each employee receives a copy. Everything from smoking rules to sick leave policies should be covered.

7. ***Expecting time to solve human conflicts.*** Passage of time can often diminish the pain that comes from a broken relationship, but time seldom solves problems. When a human relations problem surfaces, the best thing the owner can do is to sit down the party or parties involved and talk it out. Hopefully, such communication will help those involved rebuild a reward system (see Chapter 7). Left alone, most human problems will surface larger later; in the interim, the productivity of those involved will be lower.

8. ***Straightjacketing an employee.*** If you hire someone to do simple tasks, mostly running errands and clean-up work, and then decide that it is the *only* job she or he is qualified to hold, the individual will not have a chance to qualify for more responsibility. He or she will be in a psychological straightjacket, where future growth is impossible.

9. ***Discussing negative behavior of one employee with another.*** Everyone, especially a small business owner, needs to have someone to talk with about human problems. Spouses who work in the business have this advantage. An outsider, such as a CPA, can also be helpful. But talking about a problem of one employee with another is unprofessional. If you have something complimentary to say about an employee, you can say it to anyone. If the compliment gets back to the first party through the third party you talked to, all is well; the compliment is more meaningful. But, if you make a negative remark to one employee about another, and the original party hears about it, you have created a problem.

10. ***Failing to demonstrate strong leadership.*** Be a sensitive, positive, helpful team *leader* but do not become so much a part of the team that you no longer lead. Leadership (see Chapter 13) means making decisive decisions, setting visions and letting team members know when their behavior is inappropriate.

Some owners become so permissive that their employees take advantage of them. For example, a man who developed a highly successful photography shop was extremely lax in his procedures and the way he treated his staff. After ten years in business, he discovered that each month, for eight years, his most trustworthy employee, his office manager, had been stealing the equivalent of her salary. He was so upset emotionally when he made the discovery that he sold his business and retired.

11. ***Taking one of your employees for granted.*** It is difficult to explain why this happens, but many small business owners wrongfully assume that a loyal, dependable employee will continue to produce, without receiving credit. Is it because the owner believes he or she did the employee a favor when he or she was hired? Does the squeaky wheel get the attention, where the quiet, hard-working employee is ignored? Or, is it simply that the boss feels he or she has an outstanding relationship with the employee when, in fact, neglect—lack of continuous, two-way communication—has allowed it to die?

    How do you prevent this from happening? At least once each month, *check in* with each employee during a coffee break or a luncheon. Never take any human relationship for granted, especially one that is important to you and the success of your business.

12. ***Staying in the back office too much.*** Many accounting, buying, government reports, and telephoning demands can keep you in your office, away from your employees. Some of this is essential, but a common complaint from employees is that they do not get enough opportunity to communicate with their boss. Some owners make it a practice to spend a definite percentage of their time out of their offices, circulating around—serving customers, asking questions and correcting errors.

    What percentage of your time should you be spending out of your office without leaving the premises? Twenty percent? Thirty? Fifty? Keep in mind that communication is the life blood of any relationship (see Chapter 7). If necessary, *bookwork* can take place after your business is closed for the day.

13. ***Refusing to stick with your own niche.*** This may seem to be more of a marketing consideration than a human relations one. On the other hand, others—employees, suppliers, advisors—may try to convince you to expand into areas where you do not belong. *Stay with your own expertise.* It is better to do a profitable business within your own *niche* than to expand yourself into bankruptcy. It is smart to listen to others and research ideas, but when it comes time to make decisions, listen to yourself.

14. ***Failing to set collaborative goals.*** Not to involve employees in setting goals relative to the future of a business is a human relations mistake. In a sense, it is their business, too. They put their time, skills, and talents into the business. They have much to gain from the goal-setting process, as well as whether or not the goals are reached. Business goals set without comments from employees have little meaning to them; the goals are impersonal and distant. When employees have had a say in the formation of the goals, the goals become personal goals, which positively impact their day-to-day motivation. Even the productivity to part-timers can increase when they sense they are *team* members.

15. ***Keeping unsuitable employees beyond the probationary period.*** This problem, mentioned earlier, bears repeating. Over and over in my interviews with small business owners, I have been told about the damage that one unsuitable employee caused in a business. The probationary period is designed to screen out employees who can do more harm than good to your business. And, if you can get a small business owner to talk about a problem employee who was kept too long on the payroll, you will discover that the damage to the business is often less still than the psychological damage to the owner.

Your Turn   *Prioritize the human mistakes described in this chapter in order of those you feel are most apt to happen to you. Start with the mistake you are most likely to make; include those you listed on page 118.*

ASK YOURSELF

► Why is it that smart, capable people who *know* the dangers of entering into a partnership ahead of time, *still do it*?

► Discuss whether owners who claim their businesses are operating smoothly, mean all facets of the business are coordinated, or that all human relationships are healthy and free of conflict.

► CPAs and accountants can take a series of courses to upgrade their efficiency and effectiveness. How will a course in human relations result in an equivalent degree of improvement?

CHAPTER
TWELVE

HANDLING
HUMAN
PROBLEMS

THE ROLE OF COUN-SELING

In operating a small business, you will, on occasion, play the role of a coach or counselor. Counseling is talking things over with another person, to assist the individual in making a decision. Some people call the process interviewing. Sometimes you may wish to sit down with an employee and talk things over. "How are things going, Susan?" "I am pleased with your work Pedro. Is there anything I can do to make things more enjoyable for you?"

At other times, there may be a problem between you and an employee. Or, if there is a problem between co-workers, you may decide to intervene, to keep productivity high. There may be other times when an employee is doing poorly and you start the counseling process to save that employee; if things do not turn around you will, in effect, start the termination process. This chapter deals with all of these possibilities.

RULES TO FOLLOW

When a problem or personality conflict arises, either between two of your employees or between you and an employee, quick intervention is critical. Once you decide to take action, follow these rules:

RULE #1: Follow the 5 Rs of Counseling

Set up a private interview with each of the employees involved. Remember that your objective is to restore productivity (*right* purpose) at the best possible time for you and the employee (*right* time). Conduct the interview where everything will be private, and you will not be disturbed (*right* place). Approach the subject sensitively (*right* approach) and (use the *right* techniques) to make it a *win-win* situation, where both you and the employee come out ahead.

RULE #2: Your First Interview Should Be Exploratory

Initiate the communication in a non-threatening manner. As casually as possible, explain that you understand that there may be a break in the relationship between the individual and the second party, but you could be wrong. If there is a conflict, your goal is to restore the working relationship so that productivity will be restored. Nothing else. If the individual replies that there is no problem, move on to a subject in which you can pay the employee a compliment. On the other hand, if the employee admits to a relationship problem, continue with Rule 3.

RULE #3: Be an Excellent Listener

Without rushing the process, give the employee a full and free opportunity to discuss his point of view. Talk openly about it; the employee may even dissolve the problem. Or, after hearing the employee's side, you may decide that the problem will solve itself quickly and you do not need to talk with the other party.

RULE #4: Request Permission to Talk with the Other Party

If appropriate, set up a three-way interview in which you would play the role of arbitrator. If you receive permission, try to finish the interview on a high note. Say you will be in touch. If the employee is willing to solve the problem from his or her position—without involving the other party—congratulate him or her. Conclude the interview, and state that you look forward to a return to previous (or higher) productivity levels.

RULE #5: Arrange an Interview with the Other Party

State openly that you had a preliminary talk with the other party, and you would like to hear her or his side of the story. Make it clear that your goal is to resolve conflict to maintain productivity levels, and that nothing personal is involved.

Follow the 5 Rs as you set up and conduct the second interview. Once you hear the other side of the story, set up the three-way interview.

RULE #6: Take the Position of Arbitrator

Follow these steps:

▶ *Do not put the other person down.* Preserve the integrity and self-respect of all parties. It is easy to say something demeaning during a heated discussion. Avoid this by keeping your focus on the issue, not the person.

▶ *Search for common ground.* Try to see things from the other person's perspective, so that you can discover a basis to resolve the matter. To do this, listen with empathy and be flexible.

▶ *Do not expect behavioral changes.* The purpose in resolving conflicts is to find agreement on what must be done, not on whether a behavioral change is required of you or the other party.

▶ *Compromise is not throwing in the towel.* The goal is to find the best solution to improve productivity (reach agreed-upon results).

Discussing *any* problem that involves a change in behavior is sensitive. When an owner discusses a personal problem that she or he has with an employee, the situation can be even *more* sensitive. Still, you should do it. For example, if you feel you have an employee who is hostile towards you, discuss it. Hostile feelings can be dissipated through free and open discussion; when it occurs, both parties come out ahead.

Motivational Counseling

Assume you have a part-time employee who is not living up to his or her potential. You know this is true, because for the first few months after you hired this person, his or her performance was higher than it is now. You can arrange to have a non-threatening, comfortable meeting with this person to talk things over, begin something like this:

"Mary, when I hired you last June, I was confident I had employed the best person available. I still feel this way. But I sense that you are not enjoying your work like you did at the beginning. If I have done something to upset you, I'd like to talk about it. In a small operation like this, everyone on the team is important and we need your skills and enthusiasm. Can we talk about it?

The idea is to strengthen your relationship with Mary, and to help her restore her high productivity level. A motivational interview often leads to a discussion of employee goals. Where is Mary headed? How can you help her? It is amazing how *just talking things over* can re-motivate an employee.

Remember that employees like to know how they stand. Even though, as a small business owner, you may not initiate a formal appraisal procedure until you have a dozen or more employees, from time to time you will want to let them know how they are doing.

You need not have had professional training to do counseling of this nature. Follow the *5 Rs*—the right *purpose*, the right *time,* the right *place,* the right *approach* and the right *techniques*—of counseling as you talk things over in your own natural, comfortable way. Be a good listener, refrain from giving advice and be a sounding board so that you can help the individual solve his or her own problem.

Your Turn *Assume you have a young, part-time employee who you feel could be more motivated.*

▶ How would you help this person set goals and become more enthusiastic about his or her work *and* studies?

Write down the procedure you would follow and what you would try to accomplish.

▶ What would be your chance of success?

Problem Counseling

The counseling process consists of four steps: (1) Listen carefully to understand all of the ramifications surrounding the problem, (2) identify the *real* problem, and get the individual to accept this as true, (3) discuss possible alternatives and (4) assist the individual in selecting and accepting a solution.

EXAMPLE

Tamae is constantly amazed at the high volume of Veronica's hourly sales. One of three part-timers, Veronica often outsells the three full-timers on a daily basis. Tamae freely admits that her fashion boutique would miss Veronica, were she to leave. Still, in recent weeks Veronica has been disturbing the other employees with her excessive personal telephone calls and socializing while on the selling floor.

Tamae intervenes, recognizing that although Veronica's sales are high, her attitude is causing some friction and lowering the productivity of others. Her talk with Veronica starts with a few deserved compliments. Tamae then introduces the problem, asking if they could work together to find a solution. Tamae listens for a long time, verifies the problem, and they discuss possible solutions. Finally, Veronica agrees to correct the problem without losing her enthusiasm.

What do you do when two employees are having a conflict between them, which is hurting productivity? Should you intervene or wait it out?

Time, alone, seldom solves human problems. Use the *productivity rule* the moment that a human problem develops within your staff, or a problem emerges between you and a staff member. This rule states that any human problem that reduces the productivity level of a single employee deserves immediate attention. You cannot afford to wait around until a human problem disappears. To protect your business, you must intervene immediately.

EXAMPLE

In a conversation one morning with a third party, Dale discovered there were hard feelings between Khanh and Raj. After a little research, it became obvious that the conflict was hurting the productivity of both individuals. On the same afternoon that he learned of the problem, Dale talked to Khanh and Raj separately, to gain additional information. On the following day, in an effort to restore the relationship, he held a three-way conference.

By the following week, the productivity levels of Khanh and Raj were up to previous levels. Dale's quick intervention had saved the business some money and kept the relationship from degenerating further.

INTERVENTION COUNSELING

Entrepreneurs give many reasons for why they delay an intervention, in the hope it will not be necessary. They feel that:

► As non-professional counselors, they may botch it up.

► The problem may be too sensitive to handle.

► Employees need time to solve their own relationship problems with co-workers.

All of these reasons, as well as many others, do not address the bigger problem of loss in productivity. In most cases, human problems escalate if intervention does not take place. Waiting around, without clearing the air, is also difficult on the owner and may reduce her or his effectiveness.

Your Turn

Do you have a good relationship with another person—employee, family member, friend—who has a problem and who you would like to help? If so, consider trying out your counseling skills by intervening in a sensitive manner. If you do, keep in mind that counseling is primarily talking things over in situations in which you are a good listener. Together, you explore options that might reduce the size or eliminate the problem. Record the results of your intervention or interview.

If you have a problem with an employee, try out what you have learned about counseling. Then, write what you did right and what changes you will make in the future.

Counseling That May Lead to a Termination

Assume that you sense a problem with an employee. You intervene and start with an exploratory, motivational interview. After talking things over, you would decide to proceed with either a *noncorrective* interview, if you hope to resolve the interpersonal conflict, or a *corrective* follow-up, if the employee is breaking rules.

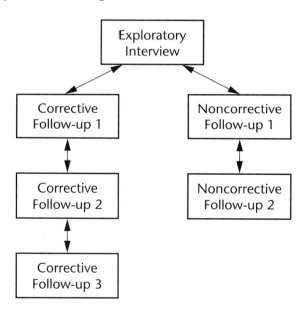

Noncorrective Follow-up 1. A single exploratory interview will not solve most human problems. It takes time to dissipate misunderstandings and misinterpretations. And, when an exploratory interview reveals hostility between the supervisor and an employee, the conflict may never be solved. But, holding one or two follow-up interviews is more effective than trying once and giving up.

EXAMPLE

Zohre, a small business owner, was disturbed when she discovered that her employee, Carol, was upset and hostile toward her. All she was able to accomplish during the exploratory interview was to listen while Carol got her inner anxieties and frustrations out in the open.

Three days later, Zohre conducted a follow-up interview that was less volatile, and was more of a two-way discussion. Both individuals admitted to some mistakes and misinterpretations. The relationship began to rebuild. Later, Zohre initiated a third interview in which they discussed mutual rewards (see Chapter 16). Eventually, the relationship was fully restored, and all hostility dissipated.

Noncorrective Follow-up 2. As illustrated above, more than one follow-up interview is often necessary to solve a human relations problem. The process of restoration is not easy or fast. In most cases, give and take is necessary to build a new foundation for mutual respect. Normally, some behavioral changes on both sides must take place between interviews. The supervisor should not expect to be able to solve all human problems, but, in most cases, the combination of good exploratory techniques plus one or more follow-up interviews will be an excellent investment to restore harmony and high productivity in a company.

An exploratory interview sometimes uncovers a serious problem, in which there has been a violation of rules. Yet, you may not have any evidence. At this point, you would set up a corrective interview:

Corrective Interview 1. This first step verifies the violation and warns the employee. Verification means gathering *critical documentation*. Although required documentation varies among businesses, it should include (1) a specific description of the violation; (2) the name of the violator, the date it occurred, and the date of the corrective interview; and (3) the written acknowledgement or rebuttal of the employee. A corrective Interview 1 is, in effect, a documented first warning.

Corrective Interview 2. This interview takes place only when a further violation is reported. If a second incident—even a different violation—is reported, the second interview uses the same documentation procedure. This meeting becomes a second warning.

Corrective Interview 3. This interview is necessary only if a third violation is reported. The procedure varies, depending on the business and its legal counsel. Generally, it includes (1) a third person in higher management, the personnel director or a staff lawyer; (2) a review and presentation of previously, documented warnings; and (3) notice of termination. Whatever the exact procedure, the business owner should promote two-way communication and attempt to show the employee that he or she has been treated fairly. The rights of the employee must be protected at all costs.

When the above procedure is followed carefully, most employees will improve their performance or submit their resignation voluntarily before Corrective Interview 3 is required.

ASK YOURSELF

▶ How will waiting to resolve human problems affect your ability as an owner-manager? That is, will carrying the problem around in your mind, instead of resolving it, make you more irritable or disturb your concentration on other problems?

▶ Many owners find it most difficult to engage in any form of counseling that may lead to a termination. What about you? Now that you know more about counseling, describe your confidence level to initiate counseling to save an employee. If it did not work, how would you start the termination process?

▶ Which would be the least traumatic problem for you to face—a financial reversal or a serious human relations problem? Discuss why.

CHAPTER
THIRTEEN

THE TEAM
APPROACH

BUILDING A CLOSE-KNIT TEAM

Bomber crews meet year after year, long after the conflict is over. Why does this happen? Members of a crew form a cohesive *team* when they know that all of their lives could depend on a single member. It is all for one and one for all.

When you start your business, you have the opportunity to build a close-knit team of your own. True, your employees will not be dependent upon you or co-workers for their lives, but being a team member has many psychological advantages. For example, when you set a goal, such as a production quota, and everyone digs in to reach that goal, a victory party is meaningful to all members; they know they have made a significant contribution. Just as bomber crews enjoy a *get together* years in the future, so can the crew of a small business. Converting your employees into a *team* may be a once-in-a-lifetime opportunity that you will not want to pass up.

Large corporations have tried for years to turn their departments into small teams that are, when properly led, more productive. For the most part, they have failed. Those who have been successful claim that:

▶ Work ceases to be just work. With more involvement, job activities take on a new flavor.

▶ Employees feel that they have been *let out of a box*. They need less supervision.

▶ Encouraging employees to be *empowered* team members gives them confidence and motivation.

▶ Teams can create loyalty.

LEADERSHIP IS THE KEY

Research shows that it takes a highly talented and sensitive person to be an effective team leader. Some business owners are uncomfortable leading a team. They fear they will lose power, that things will get away from them, and a few people will carry heavy loads, while others will waste time. While it is difficult to make a *team* work within a large organization, it is easier when one is starting a new business. Why is this true?

Because a small business either succeeds or fails *with the whole crew.* The chips are down from day one. There is no *big company* to bail you out. This realization pulls people together into a single, cohesive unit. Other reasons why a small business is ideal for the team approach include:

- ▶ Everyone has a common goal—to survive and succeed.

- ▶ Everyone is *in* on the beginning—the excitement is contagious.

- ▶ Mistakes are expected—everyone, including the owner can laugh them away and improve.

- ▶ A small business is a learning situation—everyone can participate and demonstrate initiative and flexibility.

- ▶ Victories can be shared.

Many entrepreneurs accept the advantages they have in creating a close-knit, highly productive team. However, caution is necessary. Every new owner has three basic options, discussed below. Carefully consider the advantages and disadvantages of each:

OPTION #1: The Traditional Approach

If you have been a successful manager in a situation in which authority and discipline have been effective, and you are comfortable maintaining some distance from your employees, this approach may work best for you.

In the traditional hierarchy, illustrated at the top of page 141, authority is maintained by the person in charge. Strong, two-way relationships between the owner and employees are created, but everyone knows who is the boss. The working climate is controlled. People often refer to this approach as maintaining a *tight ship.* Everyone knows what to do and the *discipline line* is well defined. Little freedom is permitted.

Some employees like a tough but fair boss, because they know where they stand. Usually, everyone produces at a high level. People take pride in their performance when high standards,

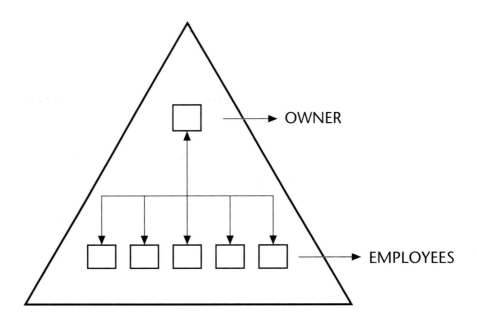

set by an authority figure, are met. As in sports, many players like a tough coach who knows what she or he is doing. Coaches who are excessively *soft* do not provide enough leadership and the team cannot stand up to pressure.

Most people like to take their automobiles into repair shops where everything is precise and orderly. They feel the owner knows what is going on and their car will be given professional care. The same is true in dental offices, hospitals and in other organizations where efficiency is respected and appreciated.

Some types of organizations do better than others, under the traditional approach. *What about your business?*

OPTION #2: The Team Approach

In this environment, the small business owner becomes a team leader. She or he is closer to team members than under the traditional, pyramid arrangement.

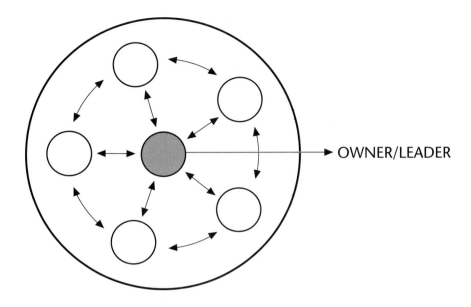

OWNER/LEADER

As the circle illustrates, the owner is in the middle, surrounded by team members who are given substantial autonomy; in short, they are expected to manage themselves, empowered to contribute more on their own terms and to *speak up* when something bothers them. Under the team approach, most decisions are made by the team. Usually everyone is involved. There is more communication, both with the owner and with the other team members. Under the circle approach, the leader—the business owner—may appear to have less authority. This is not true. Authority is simply shared more with the team members.

Behind the formation of all work teams is the idea that everyone should pull together. The goal is to make work a group effort in which everyone feels important. Two words usually come into play when thinking of the *team* approach: *collegial* means power that is shared among colleagues—team members—and camaraderie is the feeling that comes when working with people with whom you share a common condition or goal.

The benefits of a team spirit are obvious, but creating the team itself is difficult and illusive. A team leader must be positive, sensitive, concerned and patient.

OPTION 3: The Combination

Some entrepreneurs, depending upon their backgrounds and experiences, will quickly choose the traditional, structured arrangement for their own operation. Others, depending upon their age and previous experiences with the team format, will decide upon the more informal format where self-management is encouraged. Still others will recognize that they would benefit from the best of both styles:

► They will grant considerable autonomy and power to their staff, and will also maintain a strong discipline line.

► They will encourage self-management; they will back it up with frequent checks and, if needed, direct supervision.

► They will build a climate of give-and-take and, when possible, allow the team to make decisions. When the chips are down, they will move with decisive leadership.

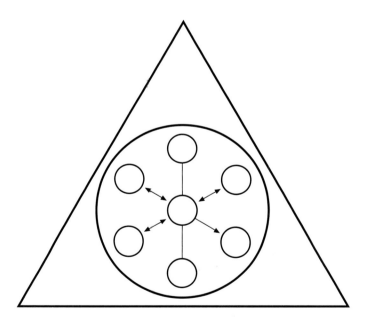

In other words, they will create an atmosphere that encourages team spirit, and they will back up this attitude with strict accountability. They will try going both ways, compromising around their own personalities, values and what works best in their business.

Your Turn

Answer the following:

► Which of the three options is best for you?

► Which approach will most effectively contribute to the profitability of your small business?

► What style best fits your own personality and type of business, and will take best advantage of your past experience?

Complete this sentence:

I will adopt the _____ for the following reasons:
                    (option)

Select the option that falls best into your comfort zone and the one that will give your business the best opportunity to succeed. Whatever your decision, incorporate the following into your approach:

► Free, open and frequent communication is essential.

► Give each employee the opportunity to be creative.

► Encourage good relationships between employees.

► Balance hard work and team successes with suitable rewards.

► Every job should have some *fun* attached to it.

► Whenever possible, give the team idea a chance to operate.

Ten Team-Building Tips

1. Talk about *our* operation or firm, rather than *my* business.

2. Share your successes and *your failures*. Having your staff go through some tough times together may help form a cohesive team, more than successful experiences.

3. Take a little time for *laughter*. The big advantage in working in a small business is that it is not necessary to view it as work.

4. If you employ one or two full-timers and three or four part-timers, *treat them all the same*. This does not mean part-timers will have the same rates of pay or benefits, but they are still team members.

5. Always give your team members full support and backing. Stand by them with their problems. Give them free time when it is vital to their lifestyles.

6. Make a habit of giving a suitable problem to every employee to solve now and then—seek their advice and follow it, or explain why you cannot.

7. Have a family *party* or picnic once a year, to tell spouses and children they are important.

8. Implement the five magical foundations in Chapter 6.

9. Try not to let a team member go home upset with you or anxious about his or her future with your firm. Talk the problem over before it becomes too big to handle.

10. Treat each team member with dignity and respect—try desperately to be fair.

ASK YOURSELF

▶ Why is it important for you to select an option that will fit into your comfort zone? Why must you be enthusiastic about your choice to make it work?

▶ Discuss why you must be true to your own personality in selecting your option.

▶ Describe how a strong, decisive leader can make the team approach work. Consider whether he or she will automatically move into a more structured approach.

CHAPTER
FOURTEEN

EXPAND
AND EMPOWER
YOUR TEAM

AFTER THE FIRST YEAR

Normally, there is some promotion when a new business opens. Invitations are mailed, advertising is scheduled. Balloons are in place. If the promotion is successful, many people stop by. Some will be customers in the future. Some will be business neighbors. Others will be suppliers. Your lawyer and CPA will probably show up. The following day, you will know that your operation has been launched and you will have, hopefully, many supporters in the days to come.

What differences will occur a year later, during your first anniversary party? In most cases, the number of people attending will have expanded many times. You will have many more customers and more employees. *And you will have built many additional relationships among people connected with your business.* Here are a few possibilities:

▶ Your lawyer, providing you have built a strong relationship with him or her, will now be a member of your team and will applaud your success.

▶ The same will be true of your CPA and tax consultant.

▶ A few of your delivery people will feel you and your business are special and that they are a part of it. One or two might offer to help with the party.

▶ You will have had time to build some mutually rewarding relationships with suppliers. If you operate a retail store, representatives of the key lines of merchandise you sell might be present. If you operate a manufacturing business, those who provide raw materials might be present.

▶ Any free-lancers, consultants or advisors you have used might attend the party.

Your list could go on and on; during the year, you will have built many supporting relationships to your business. All of these people can be considered as members of your team. All are individuals you can seek out to gain advice and suggestions. From one point of view, you can consider that you have an inside team, your employees, and an outside team, made up of people who provide support in other ways.

SPHERE OF INFLUENCE

As you think about how you might expand your list of supporters during your first year, keep in mind that each person you *convert* to your outside team has a sphere of influence. That is, they know other people who might use your products or services. Because they have some influence over these people, they might influence them to become your customers.

A successful small business is usually highly specialized. *It is also highly personalized.* In other words, the business is built upon *personal service.* Naturally, the better you serve the people in your outside support system, the more enthusiastic they will be about your business. And, as your business becomes increasingly successful, they will *brag* about knowing you and talk about how they helped you get started. All of this is the human side of operating a successful small business.

Expanding a business means building and maintaining an increasing number of human relationships, both inside and outside. When it comes to strengthening relationships outside, we are talking about *treating people better.* Naturally, when you seek advice from others and treat them as insiders by sharing *inside* information with them, they will consider themselves special and they will, in turn, keep you advised about your competitors and other information that will keep your business in front. *All lasting relationships benefit both parties.*

Your Turn   **List the kinds of outside people with whom you anticipate building strong, two-way relationships during your first year of operation. You may find it easier to list them by their positions, rather than by their names.**

EMPOWERMENT IS THE KEY TO BUILDING A STRONG EMPLOYEE TEAM

Naturally, your success in building an outside team is based upon your success in building an inside one. What is the secret to building a strong inside team? The answer may come from a single word—*empowerment!*

What is empowerment? Below is a description that will introduce you to the meaning of empowerment.

People want to make a difference, and the organization desperately needs them to. Yet, frustration results because employees, managers and organizations don't know how to take advantage of the human creativity and initiative that is there for the asking. The traditional organization needed only the bodies of employees doing their clearly defined jobs and not asking questions. Today's workplace needs employees who can make decisions, who can invent solutions to problems, who can take initiative, and who are accountable for results.

What is empowerment? **Empowerment is a fundamentally different way of working together.**

- **Employees** feel responsible not just for doing a job, but also for making the whole organization work better. The new employee is an active problem solver who helps plan how to get things done and then does them.

- **Teams** work together to improve their performance continually, achieving higher levels of productivity.

- **Organizations** are structured in such a way that people feel that they are able to achieve the results they want, that they can do what needs to be done, not just what is required of them, and be rewarded for doing so.

Scott, Cynthia D. and Scott Jaffe. *Empowerment.* Crisp Publications, Inc., 1200 Hamilton Court, Menlo Park, CA. Copyright 1991. Reprinted with permission.

The empowered workplace is characterized by:

- Enhancing the content of the work

- Expanding the skills and tasks that make up a job

- Liberating creativity and innovation

- Greater control over decisions about work

- Completing a whole task, rather than just portions of it

- Customer satisfaction

- Marketplace orientation

The empowered workplace stems from a new relationship between employees and a new relationship between people and the organization. They are partners. Everyone feels responsible for their jobs, and feels some sense of ownership of the whole. The work team is not just a reactor to demands, it is also an initiator of action. The employee is a decision maker, not a follower. Everyone feels that they are continually learning and developing new skills to meet new demands.

The key words in the above reprint are in the last two sentences: "THE EMPLOYEE IS A DECISION MAKER, NOT A FOLLOWER. EVERYONE FEELS THAT THEY ARE CONTINUALLY LEARNING AND DEVELOPING NEW SKILLS TO MEET NEW DEMANDS."

In other words, you want to employ full and part-time employees who you can *empower* to run your operation. You want employees to have a sense of ownership, whether they actually do. Treat them in a way that they feel empowered to make decisions and to show initiative.

Surveys show repeatedly that less than 50 percent of workers are satisfied with their jobs. There are many sources of satisfaction on any job; most workers do not understand them or know how to take advantage of them. For example, everyone needs to *grow*. That is, they need to learn new things, improve their skills, become more important and expand their world. When you empower an employee, you give him or her opportunities to grow. You give him or her the freedom to make decisions, learn from mistakes, submit new ideas, collaborate with others and be a true member of a team.

Glenn and Soong met for the first time when they attended a franchise school for a large corporation. They spent a week learning every possible skill that the franchisor could teach them. Both Glenn and Soong had invested the same amount of money, had similar business locations, had equivalent educations and experience backgrounds, and neither had operated a small business before.

The big difference was that Soong was a people person and Glenn was not. Soong wanted his staff to succeed and perhaps have a franchise of their own. Glenn, on the other hand, wanted to run his franchise by the book. He was more interested in his cost figures, balance sheets and management strategies than in his employees. How did things turn out? Glenn operated a model franchise and made a fair return on his investment. Soong wound up owning five franchises, all managed by people he had trained in his first operation. The basic difference is that Soong wanted his people to grow first and his business second. Thus, he took more risks with employees, empowering them to move quickly into positions of authority.

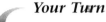

Your Turn   *Answer the following:*

► What about you? Will you operate your business *close to the vest,* or will you empower your employees to make decisions on their own?

► Will you truly give your employees a succession of growth opportunities?

Write down your philosophy toward empowerment and how you will implement your policy.

My philosophy toward empowerment is:

I intend to implement my philosophy by:

EMPOWERMENT AND TEAM COLLABORATION

Collaboration means working together as a unit or a team. Naturally, you do not want to empower members of your staff to the point they become so powerful and independent that they do not cooperate with each other. What you really want is to empower them to live up to their potential and still be good team members. A strong, successful team is more than the sum total of the power of each individual. Additional power is added when they form into a team. The check-lists below provide additional insights into how empowerment and collaboration provide the ideal team.*

When it is used well, collaboration has many benefits. In the list below, ✓ those advantages of importance to you.

❑ Collaboration builds an awareness of interdependence. When people recognize the benefits of helping one another and realize it is expected, they work together to achieve common goals. The effort is non-threatening.

❑ When people work together to achieve common goals, they stimulate each other to higher levels of accomplishment. Fresh ideas are generated and tested. The team's productivity exceeds any combined efforts of employees working individually.

❑ Collaboration builds and reinforces recognition and mutual support within a team. People have an opportunity to see the effect of their effort and the efforts of others on achievement.

❑ Collaboration leads to commitment to support and accomplish organizational goals. People gain personal power in the form of confidence when they know others share their views and are acting in concert with them.

The benefits of collaboration make it easy to understand why owners who can make it happen are considered leaders.

Team Building: An Exercise in Leadership by Robert B. Maddux. Crisp Publications, 1200 Hamilton Court, Menlo Park, California 94025. Copyright 1986. Reprinted with permission.

Collaboration can be encouraged and supported in the following ways. Check those you plan to use.

❑ Identify areas of interdependence that make collaboration appropriate. Involve team members in planning and problem solving, to help them identify where collaboration is needed.

❑ Keep lines of communication open between everyone involved in a problem, project or course of action.

❑ Let the team know, in advance, that teamwork will positively influence individual recognition.

ASK YOURSELF

▶ Do you agree that the human side of operating a small business extends to people other than employees and customers? Describe your willingness to take the time to build strong professional relationships with suppliers and others who can contribute to the success of your business.

▶ When you empower others, do you believe you also empower yourself? In other words, do you become a more powerful leader when you delegate power to others? Discuss your opinion as to whether empowerment is the key to the growth of a small business.

▶ Explain your view as to whether empowerment needs to be tempered with team collaboration to be effective. Comment on whether the team concept, in effect, places a limit on empowerment and whether teams, rather than individuals, should be empowered.

ESTABLISHING
YOUR
AUTHORITY
LINE

THE PSY-CHOLOGI-CAL ENVIRON-MENT

An authority line, sometimes called a discipline line,* is the way you control the behavior of your employees. It is the psychological climate or environment that tells employees how much freedom they have in their work stations and *what limits exist.*

Establishing the most effective authority line is more important for a business owner than a manager. An owner is absent from the premises more often, due to business and community obligations such as banking, luncheons with suppliers, attendance at service clubs. The old saying "when the cat's away, the mice will play" has a special meaning in a small business.

An authority line is also more important because, as the owner, you are more emotionally involved than a typical manager. As a result, your tolerance threshold may be lower. You might deal less objectively with an employee violation than a manager would, because your ego is more involved and you have more at stake.

In each of the following behavior areas, you have a tolerance point. This is the level where you may decide the behavior is unacceptable and step in to discuss the matter with the employee. You may be more or less tolerant in one area than another owner. Check the appropriate square to indicate your tolerance toward the following employee behaviors:

---

*Many owners and managers prefer to call what used to be known as a discipline line an authority line. The older term implies that when a violation takes place, some form of employee discipline may follow. This is not always the case.

Tolerance Exercise

	Tolerant	Somewhat Tolerant	Not Tolerant
Employee absenteeism	☐	☐	☐
Taking too long at break	☐	☐	☐
Over-socializing	☐	☐	☐
Excessive personal telephone calls	☐	☐	☐
Too many mistakes	☐	☐	☐
Inappropriate grooming	☐	☐	☐
Failure to put the customer first	☐	☐	☐
Failure to answer a telephone quickly	☐	☐	☐
Excessive fluctuations in productivity levels	☐	☐	☐
Uncooperative with co-workers	☐	☐	☐
Failure to work effectively as a team member	☐	☐	☐
Moodiness or negative attitude	☐	☐	☐
Excessive horseplay	☐	☐	☐

Your *authority line* is your general tolerance level, or the summation of all your tolerance points. It is, in effect, a line you draw that communicates what behavior is acceptable and what is not.

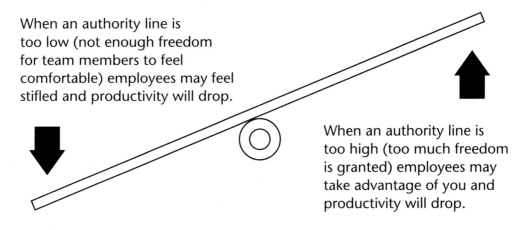

When an authority line is too low (not enough freedom for team members to feel comfortable) employees may feel stifled and productivity will drop.

When an authority line is too high (too much freedom is granted) employees may take advantage of you and productivity will drop.

Your goal is to provide just the right amount of freedom. And, equally important, to *maintain* the same authority line on a consistent basis. Some owners let their controls slip until there is too much freedom, then tighten up until there is not enough. Thus, they flip-flop; team members become frustrated and uncomfortable.

Under the team philosophy, a rather high, permissive discipline line is established *but it is still there*. Team members know it is there, and they demonstrate self-discipline. Members recognize that, to protect the freedom under which they work, they must not allow their behavior to cross the line. They must be open, professional workers who do their best without being closely supervised by the owner.

Naturally, if you establish a research laboratory and almost all of your employees are mature individuals with high academic degrees, you can form a team with a high authority line. On the other hand, if you are setting up a fast-food operation with mostly young, part-time employees, you will want a lower, but still comfortable, authority line.

How do you establish your authority line? Here are five suggestions:

1. Set a few rules that signal your low tolerance in a few selected areas. For example, you might make it a standard that you expect excellent treatment of all customers; or you might set extra high quality standards in a product you produce; or you might make it clear that you expect cooperative attitudes in working with others. You are implying that you have standards in other areas as well. Some small business owners provide each new employee with a handout that lists the basic standards expected from each employee. If it does not become too specific and list too many rules, this can be a good idea.

2. Live up to your authority line yourself. You set standards through your own behavior, which employees observe. If you violate your own standards, you raise your authority line and employees feel free to relax.

3. In staff meetings, talk about standards when you can be complimentary. Say things like "I really feel everyone is

giving the customer the kind of treatment we can be proud of." Talk about *our* standards, not *my* standards.

4. When an employee crosses your authority line a number of times, you may wish to intervene and do some *soft* counseling, in private. Make your suggestions for improvement, along with a few compliments. Never correct behavior of an employee in front of others.

5. Counsel new employees on the behaviors that are expected, so they can adjust to your authority line.

What are the characteristics of an authority line?

1. You cannot set up rules to cover all situations, so an authority line is *implied*. The few rules you do set carry over to others. For example, a strict policy on absenteeism implies a strict policy on being late.

2. Consistency is the key to an effective authority line. An owner who blows *hot* and *cold*—constantly lowering her or his authority line one day, and raising it the next—is in trouble. To be comfortable and productive, employees need to know what to expect.

3. Some flexibility is a good policy. In other words, there may be days when you relax your authority and permit different behavior. For example, many retail operations permit employees to wear costumes on Halloween.

4. Remember that a strong, consistent, yet comfortable authority line demonstrates leadership. Most employees want to be led.

At what level should you set your authority line? Here are six suggestions:

1. *Satisfy your own comfort zone first.* If you know you have a short fuse, set your line a little lower. Everyone will learn to accept and honor your standards, without frequent violations that might be emotionally upsetting. Normally, a high authority line encourages more diverse behaviors than you might be able to handle smoothly.

2. *Adjust your authority line to your special working environment.* Every type of business has its own special authority line. For example, a fast-food operation needs a low—strict—authority line. Most employees are part-timers and young, and high efficiency is required during peak periods. On the other hand, an advertising agency could have a high authority line; you are dealing with creative adults who will be more productive under a flexible and *softer* authority line.

3. It is usually a good policy to start a new business with a rather low authority line, and move higher as your standards are accepted and you determine how employees will handle more freedom. In most cases, the more freedom employees can handle, the better, as long as violations are at a minimum.

4. It is vital that an authority line be adjusted to provide the highest productivity among all employees. If you lower your line too much, you may stifle productivity; if you raise it too much, a few employees may take advantage of you. This is a delicate balance that needs to be watched carefully.

5. Keep in mind that people from other cultures expect and appreciate a lower authority line, with less freedom than is normal in the United States. People of other cultures usually produce more under a strong, lower line.*

---

*If you, as the owner of a small business, are from another culture where authority lines are usually lower, you will get the highest productivity—and retain employees—from the typical U.S. labor market if you adjust your authority line upward, and give employees slightly more freedom.

Your Turn   *In the space provided below, write the level at which you establish and maintain your authority line. Take into consideration the following factors:*

► The type of business you will operate

► The degree of customer service required

► The average age of employees

► The educational level of employees

► The need for a creative climate

► Safety factors involved

► The importance you place on quality

► Employee standards you require

► Your own personality and background

MISTAKES YOU DO NOT WANT TO MAKE

Establishing and maintaining the right authority line is a challenging goal. Regardless of how close you come to your *ideal* line that will give you the highest possible productivity, you do not want to make these mistakes:

1. Stifle creativity as well as productivity with an authority line that puts too tight a lid on your employees.

2. Lose the respect of your staff by blowing your stack in front of employees and/or customers.

3. Make big swings between a high authority line one day and a low one the next. Your goal is consistency. Should you decide to lower or raise your authority line, do it slowly so that it will hardly be recognized.

4. Refuse to consult with your staff. This can result in hanging on to a standard that is doing more harm than good for your business. Review your authority line occasionally to prevent such a possibility.

If you hire a general manager to operate your business, make sure that she or he reflects and maintains *your* authority line. Give the manager the authority to operate the business during your absence, but retain the responsibility. To accomplish this goal, provide the training required and do your best to transfer the sensitivity you have developed.

How can you maintain the best authority line for the profit of your business? Here are a few suggestions.

1. *Absorb most of the pressures that you receive from the outside, without passing them on to your employees or team members.* Some owners reflect and pass on pressures to the point that their authority line is like a yo-yo. When things get tough—for example, if financial problems arise—they lower their lines; when things look good—for example, when they receive a profitable report—they raise their authority lines and allow things to become too permissive. Under this unsettled work environment, workers do not know what to expect. As a result, their productivity drops and they seek employment elsewhere.

   This is not to say that you should absorb *all* pressures. Sometimes it is necessary to communicate whether your business is successfully competing with others, how your operation compares to others, and why it is necessary to get full productivity from all team members. Employees need to know how they are doing, and they need to know how your business is doing. You cannot form a *team* without keeping team members informed. The point is that during all up and down changes, you should keep your discipline line as consistent as possible. When things are not going well, you cannot afford to take it out on your staff.

2. *The way you react to changes and communicate them to your employees is critical to a productive climate.* The winds of economic and social change continue to blow strongly in

the United States. To survive, your business must adjust to these changes. This requires constant communication on your part. There are many reasons for doing this. First, unless your employees know how your business is doing, they will feel insecure and not know your goals. Second, they may misinterpret the facts and start rumors that could hurt your operation. Third, they need to make their own adjustments; they depend upon you to help them do this.

3. *Demonstrate that you can handle emergencies without blowing your top.* The moment you over-react to an unexpected situation, you tighten up your authority line, even without intending to do so. Employees will quickly back away from you. They will often react in an emotional and negative way themselves. When you keep your *cool* you will earn the respect of others and your authority line will remain at a more appropriate level.

4. *Your consistency eventually shows up on the bottom line.* Owners who operate their businesses on a steady, efficient, productive level, without excessive personnel turnover and human conflicts, are the ones who will show a profit at the end of each financial period. Those who blow hot and cold, with constant personnel replacements, soon discover that human relations directly influence profit.

5. *There are advantages to a moderate, firm line.* Owners who are able to strike a comfortable, but strong authority line usually come out ahead. Employees know what to expect, productivity is steady, and human conflicts are at a minimum. Keep in mind that a lower, tighter line is better than one that frustrates part of your staff. The fewer rules the better in most situations, but the rules must be clear and reasonable. Keep in mind that your line is a reflection of your leadership, and it is better to err in favor of strong than weak leadership.

6. *Check your authority line in somewhat the same way you check your sales figures.* You cannot maintain a good working climate without giving it some personal

attention. When the working climate begins to drag and your staff begins to sag, jazz things up a little. Spend some time rebuilding the positive attitudes of your employees. Have a brief end-of-the-day party. Should your staff become over-social and too relaxed, move around the work area in such a manner that they recognize that productivity needs a boost. If necessary, do some motivation counseling.

7. *The ideal climate encourages self-motivation.* When you create just the right working climate, employees will be self-motivated and productivity will be high. Your authority line will be at a good level and employees will be living up to their potentials. Your staff will be operating as a *team* and everyone will be pushing toward the same goal.

It is not easy to keep employees challenged. It is not easy to build loyalty and respect. It is not easy to bring a small operation together, so that all elements are operating in high gear. When they do, entrepreneurs recognize that the people side of their business is truly the key to their success.

Your Turn

Assume there are three ideal locations for a successful beauty shop that does hair styling, weaving, coloring, shampoo and set, manicuring and pedicuring. Assume further that the owners are highly skilled in all areas, that the shops have eight stations, and that every operator works on a commission. The owners' goals are to attract and keep customers to the point they come back and bring others, and to create a family atmosphere *in which operators and customers enjoy themselves. All three of the owners start from scratch with the same new equipment:*

▶ Jill, Owner #1, decides to operate with very high standards and a low authority line. No coffee or cookies are to be served. She imposes a dress code on all operators. Jill has a high turnover of operators and the business never gets fully off the ground.

▶ Jane, Owner #2, goes to the opposite extreme. Her policy allows each operator to *do her own thing.* She sets few standards. Her primary goals are to satisfy customers and make money. Jane devotes much of her time to resolving conflicts and her business fails after one year.

▶ Juanita, Owner #3, carefully recruits eight operators who are willing to set high standards of operation for the benefit of all. Each understands that a *team approach* will benefit operators and customers alike.

When all operators have been recruited—most are from competing shops—three meetings are held during the evening, to set standards. Everyone agrees that Juanita is the owner and leader and has the final authority to enforce standards. At the end of the three meetings, a series of work standards are approved by all operators. In other words, they pretty much set their own authority line. Juanita has the authority and responsibility to maintain the line in a consistent manner. Any major changes in the standards will be accomplished by a group meeting of all operators and the receptionist, with Juanita in charge.

Answer the following:

▶ Will this approach create a successful business for Janice?

▶ What are the good and bad features?

▶ What additions would you recommend?

ASK YOURSELF

▶ How do you reconcile the authority line you intend to establish with your efforts in building a team?

▶ What can you do to keep from blowing *hot* and *cold,* as far as your authority line is concerned? Comment on whether this means you will need to *take a walk* at times.

▶ Describe the relationship between authority lines and productivity. Why do some workers produce more under a lower line than others? How will you strike the middle ground with your employees, to achieve the highest level of productivity?

CHAPTER SIXTEEN

SEVEN HUMAN RELATIONS STRATEGIES

ASSESS YOUR PERFOR- MANCE

When we think of strategies, we normally think of financial or marketing fields, not of human relations. Yet, the term is equally applicable to the way we deal with human situations. This chapter presents strategies that have special significance to small business operators.

Rate the way you anticipate you will perform in each category. Write a number from 1 (the lowest rating you could give yourself) to 10 (the highest rating you could give yourself) in the box that precedes each strategy.

See Relationships First, Personalities Second

You will take a major step in building better relationships and avoiding damaging conflicts if you learn to concentrate on the relationship, *not* on the personality at the end of the relationship line.

EXAMPLE

Hank was pleased when he negotiated a favorable contract with a primary supplier. He was, however, upset over the personality of the delivery person, who was loud, sloppy and too free with advice. As a result, Hank concentrated on the favorable facts—that deliveries were made on time and were always top quality. Soon, the delivery person seemed to adjust to the environment Hank was trying to create. After a few months, a strong relationship was built. Later, the delivery person gave Hank advice that he needed, and which could not have come from another source.

The most objective way to view human interaction is to concentrate on the relationship itself—consider it to be a conduit or connection between people—and try to forget the personalities on either end. When you focus on the relationship and do not worry about the personalities, you can be more objective.

Some people find this impossible to do. As a result, they are unable to get beyond personality traits they consider irritating. As a result, a personality conflict often develops, and the productivity of both parties and those surrounding them is unnecessarily damaged.

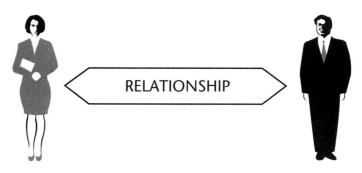

RELATIONSHIP

Although relationships usually reflect the personalities at each end of the *line,* concentrating on the relationship itself will help one ignore irritating mannerisms and concentrate instead on the potential productivity of the interaction. This concentration on the relationship instead of personalities also helps some people minimize differences in age or values, ethnic backgrounds or sexual orientation. Too often these factors negatively affect an individual's ability to see the *bigger picture.* When one pushes such matters aside and deals exclusively with the relationship itself, greater objectivity and fairness results and things move in a more positive direction.

It is a difficult lesson to learn, but if a person allows the personality of another to irritate him or her into a negative attitude, it is that individual who suffers. Away from work, we base personal relationships on personality. In the workplace, however, where productivity hinges on positive relationships, it can be a different matter.

To keep work relationships in good order, it is best to observe what people do, rather than what they seem, on the surface, to be. Work habits are often far more important than personality differences. Entrepreneurs who deal with working relationships and not personalities do themselves and their business a favor.

 *Your Turn*   *Describe a situation in which you intensified a human relations problem because you allowed a personality characteristic of another to overshadow his or her performance and, as a result, failed to build a healthy relationship with the individual.*

Practice the Mutual Reward Theory

When it comes to handling a one-on-one session with an individual with whom there is a conflict, a direct approach is not always the best. For many people, a confrontation may be too stressful and uncomfortable. A better plan may be to initiate a discussion that develops a MUTUAL REWARD approach.

The Mutual Reward Theory (MRT) states that for a human relationship to remain healthy over an extended period of time, the benefits should be somewhat equal between both parties. What is important is that each participant views what she or he receives from the relationship as *satisfactory*. Both individuals should feel they come out ahead. The idea is to introduce the *mutual reward* concept with the other party.

EXAMPLE

Joan, sensing that her relationship with Kathleen—her only full-time employee—was deteriorating, invited Kathleen into her office and said, "Up until now, we have really been partners in this business, but I get the feeling we are beginning to work against each other instead of pulling together. If I am at fault, I would like to make any changes necessary. Can we sit down and work out a better reward system? Perhaps there is something I should do to make your work more enjoyable."

Using the mutual reward idea is a good idea, because it takes an oblique, rather than confrontational approach. Not only is it easier to use, but with open communication a more satisfactory reward mix usually develops. In almost all relationship conflicts, reconciliation depends upon the creation of a more satisfactory reward system. This is the true meaning of *give-and-take* or *compromise* in conflict resolution.

Your Turn   ***Using MRT counseling, you can strengthen a relationship with another by sitting down and discussing—sometimes listing—the actual rewards that each party is receiving from the other. This process often uncovers new rewards that each party can provide the other, thereby improving the relationship. Try MRT counseling and write the results below.***

☐ Let Small Irritations Pass

How many times have you seen someone come away a winner who made a fuss over slow service in a restaurant or complained to a postal employee? Did the individual really win when telling somebody off on the telephone or becoming angry in a traffic jam? Or, worst of all, when exploding in the work environment?

EXAMPLE

Years ago, my wife and I were waiting for a valet to bring our car to the front of a restaurant where we had enjoyed a delightful dinner. When the car arrived, I noticed a large dent in the rear fender. I immediately blew my top. After embarrassing both my wife and myself, we discovered the valet had brought another customer's car that was identical to ours. Our car was fine. I did not sleep well that night, but it was my fault. I had blown my stack before I properly assessed the situation. I had victimized myself.

You might feel it is good to *blow off some steam*, but in most cases similar to the above, a *short fuse* person either hurts his or her image, or winds up embarrassed and feeling foolish. Even worse, if you *blow up* over a minor irritation that was nobody's fault and then recognize it later as being *dumb*, it can ruin the rest of your day. The truth is, even though your complaint may be justifiable, *you* become the victim, not the other party. How can you prevent this from happening?

► Work on detaching yourself emotionally from the upsetting trivia of operating your business. Refuse to let an employee, customer or vendor *get under your skin.*

► Train yourself to look beyond small incidents that do not, in the long run, have a negative impact upon you or your business. Remind yourself that being a *picky* owner makes both you and your business *smaller* in the eyes of others.

► Quickly remind yourself that emotional upsets of any kind turn you—not your employees, customers or vendors, but *you*—into a victim.

Choose Advisors Carefully

Every successful owner has a few reliable advisors. Some, such as lawyers and tax experts, are paid for their services. Others, such as suppliers, teachers and friends who own their businesses provide suggestions because they want you to succeed.

Because of their highly independent nature, many entrepreneurs are reluctant to seek and accept advice from others. Sometimes it boils down to sheer stubbornness. Obviously, this attitude becomes a serious barrier to the success of any business. Few, if any, business owners have all of the correct answers. Each owner, at times, needs to back away and listen to others who can be more objective and provide a better answer to a problem.

When relationship conflicts develop, there is a critical need to talk things over with others who can be objective. This is also therapeutic. Whom should you select? Upon what basis?

Common sense tells us that it is smart to keep *home based* problems away from work and some work problems away from home. This is especially true when you need to discuss a conflict involving a co-worker or family member. For example, unless you have an outstanding relationship, it is probably best to talk over a serious work conflict with a mature outsider (spouse, friend or professional counselor). On the other side of the coin, talking freely about a home problem with co-workers may hurt productivity or your image and possibly damage your relationships at home, especially if word gets back that you have been discussing details of your home life.

The problem comes in selecting the *right* person to assist you, who can provide objectivity. Those closest to you may be your logical first choices, but if they are not objective, taking their advice could do more harm than good.

So what is the answer? Use discretion!

Choose your *confidants* carefully so your problem will not spill over and disturb other relationships, at home or at work. The following suggestions may help:

1. Select an advisor who is far enough removed from the problem to be objective.

2. Try not to settle for any *advice* unless all parties in the conflict stand a chance of coming out ahead.

3. Be true to yourself and to your judgment.

4. If you receive assistance from a friend, consider the help you receive a gift, and try to return it in the future.

Top executives of large corporations can call in professional, paid consultants when solving a major problem. Small, independent owners may find it necessary to discuss a problem with a friend or supplier who is in a position to act as a non-paid consultant.

☐ Know When To Compromise

The owner of a small business has the final say when it comes to solving human relations problems. Compromise is seldom necessary. Yet, in many or most situations, it is the smart thing to do.

EXAMPLE

Janet became so upset with Tracy, the most productive employee in her flower shop, that she was tempted to work out an agreement to pay Tracy off financially, to eliminate the conflict between them. Then, Janet talked to her lawyer and decided that a better solution would be to resolve the conflict and restore their relationship.

What did the lawyer say to change her mind? "Janet, if you terminate Tracy, it could turn out to be very expensive. But that isn't the only reason you should seek a compromise. The truth is that you need her—nobody can touch her talent in the field of flower designs. You have told me this yourself. So, in the long run, a simple human relations problem could turn you into the victim. Tracy could easily go to work for a competitor, which would make you the victim. It may hurt a little now, but it will not diminish your leadership to give in a little. In the end, the relationship may become stronger, and both you and Tracy will become winners instead of losers."

Sometimes compromise is smart for these reasons:

▶ It may generate new rewards that you value as much, or more, than those you lose.

▶ You may benefit when you accept new ideas in the course of a compromise.

▶ Compromise may be the *only* way to restore a relationship.

Compromising to protect our future without hurting others is smart human relations for many reasons. Here are two:

1. Conflicts that hurt others can *boomerang.*

2. Vindictive behavior is never respected by others.

☐ Communicate With Staff

Communication is the life-blood of all relationships. Misunderstandings occur when there is lack of communication and relationships often fall apart. In a small business partnership, frequent communication between partners is critical. When there is a single owner, communication with all employees is essential. Communication is also vital between customers, suppliers and advisors. The owner of any small business who spends too much time behind the scenes with the financial side of the operation, and too little time with his or her people, will eventually get into trouble.

When he opened his repair shop, Jerry quickly got the message that he needed to build relationships with people and communicate daily with his mechanics and suppliers. But Jerry enjoyed working with his computer. Most of the time, his office door was closed, while Jerry did financials, reports and government reports. He thought he was communicating, when he was not!

After coming close to bankruptcy, Jerry started to realize that bookwork came second, after sales and communication, the foundation upon which sales and profit are based. It took him one year to understand how significant communication can be in a small business.

Today, you will find Jerry out in the front of the store, dealing with customers and employees. He delegates some of the bookwork to an assistant, and does what he must do himself at night.

☐ Be a Superior Listener

It is said that one must have a strong ego to be successful as the owner of a small business. That is, he or she should always be in charge and willing to make tough decisions. This does not mean, however, that you should make decisions without involving others. It really means that you *find* the answers, listening to others. Then, you act, giving credit as you go.

No one person has all the answers. The entrepreneur who *knows it all* will, sooner or later, make too many mistakes to survive. Operating any small business today is far too complicated for one person to have all the answers.

What is the answer, then? The answer lies in going to those who know more about a specific area, and following their advice carefully. This takes the willingness and the ability to be a good listener.

Your Turn   *List the seven human relations strategies presented in this chapter, in the order that you rated them.*

      1.

      2.

      3.

      4.

      5.

      6.

      7.

Circle the strategy that you feel you need to improve the most.

ASK YOURSELF

▶ When you find yourself in a human relations conflict with another person, what can you do to improve your communications strategy?

▶ Some people say that MRT is nothing more than "you scratch my back and I'll scratch yours." How would you convince such a person that MRT is much more?

▶ Why might it be more difficult for an entrepreneur to compromise than for an employee to compromise?

CHAPTER SEVENTEEN

SMALL BUSINESS AND THE TELEPHONE

THE HEART OF COMMU-NICATION

It is easy to say that the telephone is the small business owner's best friend. It is true, of course, but it is also an understatement. The telephone is more than a best friend, it is the heart of the entire communication system.

► Through the telephone, customers can be attracted and served and problems can be solved.

► Properly used, the telephone gives the owner and staff access to suppliers, professional advisors, agents, distributors, etc.

► Today, far more than in the past, business is done over the telephone. If the telephone was the small business operator's friend ten years ago, it is now his or her partner.

It has become too expensive for a wholesaler or middle-man to meet clients face-to-face, *on a regular basis.* Today, everyone appreciates a face-to-face meeting, but no longer expects it. The telephone has changed the way America does business, and the entrepreneur must take advantage of it. Those who are successful do just that!

This chapter will show you how to make the most of your telephone system, whatever it may be. Your first source should be the telephone company. Simply call your telephone company and ask for all of the assistance they can provide— technical advice, help in training your staff, etc. Then consider these suggestions:

► Teach your staff the best use of the telephone, by being a model user.

• Do not eat or drink while you talk on the telephone. If you must, excuse yourself and then, quickly, swallow and start over.

• Answer the phone as soon as possible. A maximum of three rings is a good standard.

• Should you place a caller on hold, ask for permission: be sure you receive a favorable answer. An abrupt "please hold" is not the best way to handle this situation.

- Place the caller on hold before discussing his or her situation with a co-worker. You will lose any customer or supplier who hears you say something negative, not meant for his or her ears.

▶ Instruct your staff to put smiles in their voices. It may sound like an over-simplification, but on the telephone you can *hear* a smile. This will help to improve communication on the telephone, and the habit will help in direct contact with customers.

▶ Conduct a ten-minute session with your staff on how to take telephone messages. Follow these suggestions:

- *Get the first and last name of the preson calling.* If the name is unusual or unfamiliar, ask the person to spell his or her name, too. This will ensure that the message will have accurate information. Do *not* ask the caller, "Does he (or she) know you?"

- *Get the name of the organization.* This will provide a useful reminder for the recipient of the message and if an error was made when taking down the phone number, it will serve as a way to double-check the correct number.

- *Save call-back time.* Ask the caller if there is a message or any information he or she would like to leave. This will save time for the person for whom you are taking messages.

- *Tell the caller that you will give the person the message.* Use the professional, *"I'll ask Mr. Lee to call you."* End your call with, *"Thank you."*

- *Record the date and time of the call on the message.* Include your name or initials in case the recipient has any questions about the message.

► Improve your own effectiveness on the telephone—and save time—by following these suggestions:

Incomplete or partial messages are a major source of wasted time and frustration. You can save time and stress for the person you call—and for yourself—if you hone your message-giving skills by practicing the following tips:

- *State your first and last name and the name of your organization.* Do not try to make the person guess your name from the sound of your voice. It takes only a moment to give the information and saves the caller and you time.

- *Give the caller your phone number.* They may have your number and call you every day, but not everyone memorizes all their frequently called phone numbers. Distractions or pressing matters can easily cause a brief lapse in memory, so extend the recipient the courtesy of giving them your phone number without being asked.

- *Avoid run-together phone numbers.* A string of rapidly stated numbers is confusing and increases the chance of message-taking mistakes. You will save the time of having to repeat numbers if you slowly state your phone number, starting with the area code. Pause between each group of numbers. For example, say, *"Area code two-four-two (pause), five-five-five (pause), six-one-two-one."*

- *Leave a message that explains why you need a return call.* If the recipient needs to get information for you, this will save them the time of calling you and finding out that there was information they needed to get, then calling you again with the information.

Your thoughtfulness in giving complete telephone messages will be appreciated and save time for all involved.

TELEPHONE EFFECTIVENESS REVIEW

You already know how important the telephone will be to the future of your enterprise. That is why, undoubtedly, the moment you knew you were going into business you listed your firm in the local telephone directory. You may have also decided to pay for a small ad in the classified section. You can double the effectiveness of your telephone if you use it to its full advantage. Here are three rules to follow to improve your image when using the telephone:

▶ ***Rule 1:*** Always answer the telephone in a positive manner. Give your name and the name of your firm, and ask, "How may I help you?" Many people say if you smile to yourself as you pick up a telephone, you convey a *warmer* welcome. It is also important to answer the telephone promptly—many firms take pride in having employees answer within three rings.

▶ ***Rule 2:*** Once you learn the reason for the call, make sure you either satisfy the customer yourself or turn him or her over to the proper person without losing the party on the line. That is, see that the right party is reached and do not keep the individual on *hold* any longer than necessary. If you receive a second incoming call while talking with a customer, ask to be excused while you put the person on hold.

▶ ***Rule 3:*** If you handle the call completely yourself, wind up the contact by seeing that the customer is fully satisfied. If you were unable to solve the problem, ask the individual to call again so that you will have another chance to be of service. Always conclude with: "Thank you for calling us" or another appropriate and pleasant remark.

Your Turn   *Based upon your experience using the telephone in business and the material you have just read, complete the following form to be used by all employees in your operation:*

Telephone Guide

1. Always answer the telephone by saying: _____

   _____

   _____

2. If the party the caller wishes to talk with is not available say: _____

   _____

   _____

3. If the caller wishes to leave a message, follow these six rules: (see page 186).

   (1) _____

   (2) _____

   (3) _____

   (4) _____

   (5) _____

   (6) _____

   Make sure the message is placed on the desk of the individual the party is trying to reach.

4. Answer calls before the telephone rings more than _____ times.

5. Always smile when you answer a telephone, so that your voice will communicate _____.

6. If you ask an outside party to hold, be sure you get back to the party within _____ seconds.

7. If you cannot correctly answer a question for the caller, tell the caller that you will ask me to call back within _____.

8. Always say _____ _____ or _____ at the termination of a call.

9. _____

(other suggestions from you)

10. _____

(other suggestions from you)

ASK YOURSELF

▶ How much time do you anticipate you spend on the telephone on a normal business day?

▶ If you discover one of your employees is not being as friendly and effective on the telephone as your standards require, what steps will you take?

▶ How prepared are you to be a model telephone user?

CHAPTER EIGHTEEN

IMAGE
BUILDING

SELLING YOURSELF

This chapter looks at the human dimensions of selling your products and services, your business as an entity, and yes, *selling yourself.* It does not teach selling techniques.

Using the baseball diamond again to present what is involved in selling products and services, we will compare selling a product or service with selling your business (image) as well as yourself.

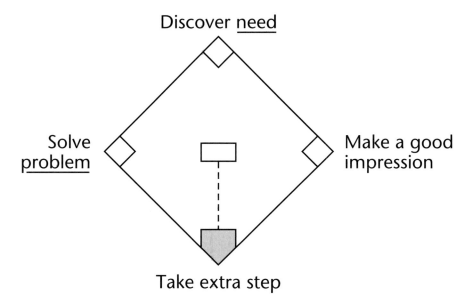

Discover <u>need</u>

Solve <u>problem</u>

Make a good impression

Take extra step

Selling Your Products and Services

You get to first base when you make a good impression with the customer or client, both in person and on the telephone. You want to present a neat, clean and efficient image. In doing this, you and your employees want to transmit a feeling of friendliness.

Once you accomplish this, you are ready to take the client to second base. How do you do this? You discover the *need* the customer came to you to satisfy. Once you discover that you are in a position to satisfy the need—you have the product or expertise—then you are ready to take the client to third base. If you cannot satisfy the need, suggest where the client can find another quality business, better equipped to serve him or her.

To get to third base, you must satisfy the need or solve the problem he or she brought to you. Selling is problem solving. The closer your product comes to satisfying the need, the better; the more help you provide in helping the customer solve his or her problem, the better. Consider yourself as a consultant, rather than a salesperson.

You get a client to home base—and *he or she* wins the game as you do too—when you wrap up the sale or contract and *go that extra step to do it with class.* This means providing the customer with something extra that he or she probably would not get from a competitor—*something he or she will remember.* It could be anything from a personalized comment, wrapping a product in a special way, making a follow-up telephone call or, as they sometimes do in candy shops, giving the customer a special chocolate to enjoy now.

From your perspective as the owner, selling a specific product or service is vastly different from selling your enterprise as an isolated business, and also from selling yourself as a personality. The baseball analogy, however, still works.

SELLING YOUR IMAGE

You get to first base when you introduce yourself *as the owner* and communicate to the client that it will be an honor to personally serve her or him. Make the customer feel important.

You reach second base when you convince the client that you and your business are in the best position to serve her or him—you intend to give more personal attention than competitors.

You arrive at third base when the customer is convinced that she or he has found the right small business *to do business with*—no problem is too small or too big for you to handle.

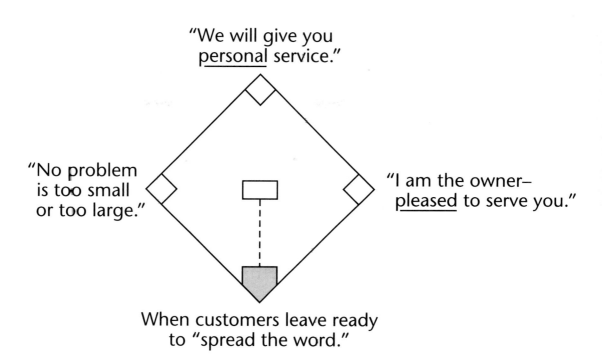

"We will give you <u>personal</u> service."

"No problem is too small or too large."

"I am the owner– <u>pleased</u> to serve you."

When customers leave ready to "spread the word."

You get to home base and score a run when the client leaves with such an upbeat impression that she or he will spread the word in the community. This also means that when the client returns, he or she will seek you out, remember your name and feel that you are a special friend upon whom the individual can rely.

All of this may sound like you are *tooting your own horn* too much and going overboard with personal service. Not so! Remember that your personal service is something that bigger operations cannot provide. It is, therefore, your most effective competitive weapon. *The truth is that most small businesses are built around the personality of the owner.* That is why many small business operations are named for the owner. And, you will notice, almost always the first, more informal, name is used.

Word of Mouth

If you talk to an advertising specialist, she or he can never tell you exactly what it costs to attract—through advertising alone—a single customer. You can be sure, however, that those who are attracted 100 percent by word-of-mouth cost you nothing. A fully satisfied customer—you took that extra step—not only comes back to you again and again, but he or she brings others.

Mary and her husband Jake decided to open a small cafe in a new industrial park where they would only serve breakfasts and lunches. Although they made sure their business would be listed in the next telephone directory, they engaged in no other advertising. It was their conviction that if they opened without fanfare, and made certain that each customer left psyched up to tell others, they would prosper. How did it work out? Within five months they had all the business they could handle. Mary and Jake are convinced that word-of-mouth *is the most powerful form of advertising and public relations.*

A small business cannot afford a single dissatisfied customer. Why? Because one unhappy customer multiplies geometrically and can reduce the size of your trading area. Your trading area is the distance from your business—in all directions—that you can hope to attract clients. Are you confined to one neighborhood in a large city, everyone in a small city, or can you hope to attract clients from outlying areas or even other cities, some distance away?

Your Turn

What is your* trading area? *How far in all directions do you hope to attract people? Get a map and draw a circle that extends in all directions,* as far as you can reasonably expect to draw or serve customers. *If you have a local, community newspaper—daily or weekly—you may decide that your trading area is the same one the newspaper serves. If so, you are in luck, because your trading area is already defined. If a map is not easily available, fill in the circle on the next page to indicate your location and the distance from which you intend to draw customers. Keep reminding yourself that it is within this circle that you will concentrate your image building.

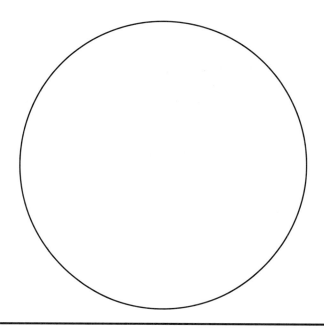

EMPLOYEES CAN EXPAND YOUR TRADING AREA

So far in this chapter we have been talking about customers. What about employees? When you start a small business and you are the owner, everyone is, in effect, *your boss*. It is more important that you make them happy than it is for them to satisfy you. Why? Because they will be talking about their job to all of their friends.

Every employee, as is true of customers, has a sphere of influence. Most can have a positive influence on those within their sphere. For example, if an employee is happy and excited about his or her job, the individual will talk about it to others. Curiosity will set in and these people will want to visit your operation. All of this is exactly what you want. You want to attract people without paying for it directly. We say some leaders have a mystic or charismatic aura surrounding them; you want to create the same around your business.

Just as you wish to create strong and supportive relationships with customers and employees, you want to do the same with suppliers. People who provide services to you and your business are key as you build the image of your firm. Just as you will be smart to take *that extra step* with clients and employees, taking it with suppliers is equally important. They own a different sphere of influence, which can impact your business' success in many ways.

HANDLING UPSET PEOPLE

Because people often have their own problems and frustrations, they are sometimes difficult to deal with. How do you protect your business image when you handle unreasonable customers and others who are unhappy? Here are three rules to follow:

▶ ***Rule 1:*** Listen carefully to their complaints. Write down the specifics as they talk. Do not interrupt until they have had ample time to let off most of the steam that has built up within them. Like a balloon losing air, by talking people will sometimes deflate their own objections.

▶ ***Rule 2:*** At the appropriate time, ask: "What will it take to make you happy?" This puts the complaint back in their court. In most cases, it will not take a great deal to satisfy them.

▶ ***Rule 3:*** If their request is within reason, do it. Keep in mind that your purpose is to convert them from unhappy people to happy so they will tell others how fairly they have been treated. This may mean going a little further than you anticipated. Your goal is not just to get the individual *off your back;* it is also to make this person a *salesperson* for your organization.

This chapter includes many suggestions on how *you, the owner* can work with customers, employees and suppliers to build a better image of your business. Naturally, the better job you do personally, the better any employees you have will also do. You cannot expect others to live up to your expectations without doing so yourself.

ASK YOURSELF

▶ Discuss the idea that your personality plays the key role in communicating the best image of your operation.

▶ Describe the relationship between your ability to establish a powerful, positive image and the size of your trading area.

▶ Discuss your willingness to base the future of your operation primarily upon the human relationships you build and maintain with customers, employees and suppliers.

CHAPTER NINETEEN

QUESTIONS FROM THE BACK ROW

TRAIN YOUR BACKUP NOW!

Assume that you are participating in a seminar on the human side of operating a small business and the instructor has opened the discussion for questions:

How soon should I train a backup for myself, as the sole proprietor? Immediately! Even if you start out with a single part-time employee, this individual should be your backup, in case you need to leave the shop for an hour or so. As you expand, you will need a full-time assistant and a manager. Hire your first employees with this need in mind. Eventually, you will want to make sure you have selected the best possible person, one who is capable of absorbing the training it will take, that you will provide. This relationship will be the most important of all.

My husband and I are planning to open a mom-and-pop operation. Any special advice? Mom-and-pop operations have a long tradition of success. As you might imagine, there are some serious pitfalls. Here are ways to avoid three of them.

First, divide up the responsibilities according to your abilities, talents and desires. One spouse will usually be more people oriented than the other. This individual is the one who should do the employment, counseling and sales training—in other words, take over the personnel function, while the other spouse assumes other, equivalent responsibilities. Second, do all of your planning together, away from employees, so that no arguments occur in front of staff. Third, always talk over human problems that need to be solved, but have employees deal only with the owner designated to be in charge of personnel. Staff should be responsible to only one boss. Good luck.

What about employing family members? Here, again, it has been a long-standing tradition for small business owners to employ members of their families. Most of the time it works. For example, Knott's Berry Farm in California started as a family affair and pretty much continues to be so today. There are, of course, certain dangers. The number one danger is that non-family employees feel discriminated against and, as a result, their productivity drops and human relations become unhealthy. It is difficult, perhaps impossible, to be totally fair when a family member is designated to assume a management and leadership role. The warning signs are up, and some owners handle the situation remarkably well. If you intend to employ members of your family, you will need to be unusually smart and sensitive to human relations.

Should a small business owner prosecute an employee who has been proven to be dishonest? There are at least two levels of dishonesty here. If an employee is caught stealing a single, minor item, termination may be a sufficient penalty. In more serious cases, the police should be contacted, and some form of retribution should be expected. In either case, the owner must be careful not to wind up as the victim. That is, if going through the prosection process (court appearances, etc.) becomes too traumatic for the owner, a less involved process may be best.

I have a short fuse. I am fearful that I will blow up in front of my employees or customers. How can I keep my cool in difficult situations? The last thing you want to do is explode in front of your employees, a customer or a supplier. Even if in all other areas you are highly effective, the damage will be severe.

I have a friend who was, at one time, a top executive for a New York based firm. One of his problems was to control himself emotionally during staff meetings. Two conditions caused this. First, he was a decisive decision-maker and he became impatient with long, drawn-out discussions when, to him, the right decision was obvious. Second, he admittedly wore his heart on his sleeve. That is, his emotional threshold was low. He *flared up* easily when people failed to listen and wasted his time.

Recognizing these characteristics, my friend developed a highly personal executive pacifier. Having moved to New York from San Francisco, he had collected a number of small, smooth stones from a local beach. He discovered that if he held one of the stones—perhaps indented a little to fit his thumb—in his hand and rubbed it slowly, it helped him relax and provided a higher threshold of tolerance. In short, it helped him keep his emotions under control.

Owning and operating a small business can put an individual in a pressure cooker, similar to that of a corporate executive. When an individual recognizes that she or he has a *short fuse,* any device that controls emotions is worth considering. None of the other executives where my friend worked knew of his stone. He told me about it long after he retired. The point is, of course, that it worked for him. So if you would find it embarrassing to take *worry beads* or other devices to work with you, consider a small stone you can secretly hold in your hand that will help you see things in a better perspective.

Other possibilities might be:

▶ Excuse yourself and walk away.

▶ Turn the problem over to an assistant, by stating you have an emergency problem elsewhere that demands your attention.

▶ Excuse yourself for a few moments until you can spend a few moments alone and get *your emotions under control.*

Should a small business owner use formal appraisals with employees, as most big corporations do? Everyone needs some feedback every six months, on how they are doing in a job. As a small business owner, you need not start out with a complicated appraisal form, but at the least you should appraise and discuss the performance of each staff member at regular intervals. Do not delegate these appraisals until you have over twenty employees. Once you delegate, a more formal appraisal form and procedure may be in order. It will be a good idea for you to appraise yourself after you rate others, or have your spouse or CPA do it for you.

What are the three most serious human relations mistakes new small business owners make? My assessments, in order of their importance, would be: one, waiting to solve serious human relation problems; two, over-identifying with one or more employees; and three, failing to delegate more as the business expands.

Your Turn

Write three questions concerning the human side of operating a small business that you still want answered. If these questions are not answered in this chapter, discuss them with two or three experienced and successful small business owners.

Questions:

1.

2.

3.

What kind of bonus or incentive plan would you recommend for a very small business? A simple annual Christmas bonus, based upon a percentage of net profit for the year, works well. It is usually best to base the amount on whether the employee is a full or part-time employee, and the number of months he or she has been employed during the year. It should be understood by the staff that without a profit there is no bonus. As a business grows, more sophisticated profit sharing and retirement plans can be considered. Your CPA and/or tax professional can tell you the advantages and disadvantages of various possibilities.

Should I establish graduation from high school as a minimum requirement for employment? It is a good minimum standard in most labor markets, but there is nothing wrong in making some exceptions, especially for part-time employees. Also, keep in mind that different educational systems are in play in other countries. You do not want to pass up an outstanding employee from a different culture because of such differences, even if you will need to assist the individual in improving English skills.

Is good internal human relations more important today than in previous years, in the operation of a small business? Absolutely! This is true for two reasons. In the first place, better internal human relations result in greater productivity. Secondly, better treatment of employees is increasingly mandated by government laws. When you follow good human practices, you avoid discrimination and no law suits will follow. You will avoid sexual harassment of any kind. Today, employees know their rights; any small business operator who violates the rules—minimum wages, regular fifteen minute breaks every four hours, overtime pay, etc.—is inviting trouble.

What are the advantages in establishing good human relations in a small business? There are many advantages. Here are three to keep in mind. First, when you treat your employees with care and sensitivity, they will, in turn, give co-workers and customers better treatment. Second, it is impossible to build a smoothly operating *work team* without practicing good human relations. Third, as we have stated repeatedly, practicing good human relations is a *win-win* philosophy. When you practice good human relations, everything benefits—especially your business.

What if you inadvertently employ an alcoholic or drug user who is disruptive to your organization? Follow these steps: First, with a third party present, meet with the employee to discuss the problem (document this and all other meetings). Second, recommend rehabilitation as a requirement to keep his or her job. Third, if immediate improvement is not forthcoming, issue a second warning that further evidence will result in a notice of termination. Fourth, give formal notice of termination and inform the employee that you have documented the previous meetings.

What is the best time to counsel a problem employee? Late in the work day, but still on your time. Give him or her a short notice that you want to meet, perhaps an hour, so that the productivity of the individual will not deteriorate further before the meeting. Make sure the meeting takes place in private, away from other employees. When a meeting is required to protect your own peace of mind, do not delay. Time alone seldom causes a problem employee to improve.

How would you handle a rumor that is circulating and hurting productivity? Call a staff meeting immediately. Confirm or squelch the rumor. For example, if you were in the process of negotiating a lease to move your business to a new location, you would want to provide some details. If the rumor was false and you were not negotiating, you would say so.

What are the human rewards to owning your own business? Whether employees remain with you or not, you can establish many rewarding, life-long relationships. You have the option to build a business *family* in which children of employees, including your own, can seek employment at an early age. You will be in a position to help members of your own family, employees, customers and members of your community over some *rough spots*. Many entrepreneurs make quiet but significant contributions to the lives of others. Their roles as community leaders make this possible.

What other sources of information are available regarding the human side of operating a small business? An excellent source is the Small Business Administration. Write SBA Publications, P.O. Box 30, Denver, Colorado 80201-0030 for a directory of publications and videotapes. Do not forget your public library or commercial bookstore. Both usually have a section devoted to entrepreneurship. To start out, you might wish to check the Crisp Publications at the back of this book.

ASK YOURSELF

▶ If you were given your choice to be exceptionally strong in two of the areas listed below, and measurably weaker in the remaining area, which would it be? Why?

- The financial aspects of operating a business

- The human side of operating a business

- The marketing side of operating a business

▶ Discuss your position in regard to nepotism.

▶ How can your kind of personality be used to an advantage in your business?

CHAPTER
TWENTY

YOUR ROLE
AS A
LEADER

DO YOU HAVE THE RIGHT STUFF?

When an individual decides to start a small business, she or he is saying: "I am a leader. I will step out in front and establish a business that will eventually be ahead of competition, and it is my responsibility to lead my employees in that direction."

Do you have the right stuff to be a leader? You have already demonstrated you do by making the decision to own and operate a business of your own. You are willing to take the risk. You are anxious to put it together. To put it more directly, entrepreneurs have leadership instincts, whether they recognize them or not. *The potential is there.* It is not a matter of whether or not you have the right stuff, but whether you can develop what is within you.

Keep in mind that we are talking about being a good leader, and not a good manager. There is a big difference. A *manager* is a person who can control an operation and keep it running smoothly. A manager makes use of all resources to create a profit. A manager is a coordinator. A leader, on the other hand, is first a good manager, and she or he is also a good leader. One who manages well is free to lead; that does not mean he or she accepts the challenge of leadership.

This chapter will help develop your innate leadership qualities. First, it is a good idea to measure your leadership potential. This will give you an idea of how important leadership is, and how far you have to go.

Leadership Potential Scale*

HIGH LOW

	HIGH								LOW		
I can be both an excellent manager and have time to lead.	10	9	8	7	6	5	4	3	2	1	I am satisfied with being a good manager.
I am a visionary. I love to plan for long-term goals.	10	9	8	7	6	5	4	3	2	1	Getting by one day at a time is my goal.
Risk-taking is my cup of tea. It challenges me.	10	9	8	7	6	5	4	3	2	1	I avoid risks whenever possible.
It is a challenge to discipline others.	10	9	8	7	6	5	4	3	2	1	I do not enjoy having to discipline others.
I enjoy communication and have the potential to become outstanding.	10	9	8	7	6	5	4	3	2	1	My communication skills are adequate.
I have the desire to become a top leader.	10	9	8	7	6	5	4	3	2	1	I am comfortable as a follower.
I enjoy making tough decisions.	10	9	8	7	6	5	4	3	2	1	Decisions can be frustrating and scary.
I seek and welcome more responsibility.	10	9	8	7	6	5	4	3	2	1	I avoid added responsibilities.
I can handle the pressure of being in the limelight, under fire.	10	9	8	7	6	5	4	3	2	1	Pressure is not for me.
I believe I have the personality to become a successful leader.	10	9	8	7	6	5	4	3	2	1	Sorry, I am not the leadership type.

TOTAL [   ]

If you scored 80 or above, it appears that you have a high desire and potential to be a leader. A rating between 60 and 80 shows good potential. A rating under 60 is a signal you may wish to delay weaving leadership practices into your management style.

What are the characteristics of leadership? There are many *personal* traits such as integrity, tact and the ability to keep cool under pressure. Personal characteristics are equally important to good managers. If the six broad characteristics illustrated as rungs on The Leadership Ladder below are developed, they will eventually determine the difference between being a good manager and a good leader-manager. You may wish to call these the *principles* or *foundations of leadership.*

The Leadership Ladder

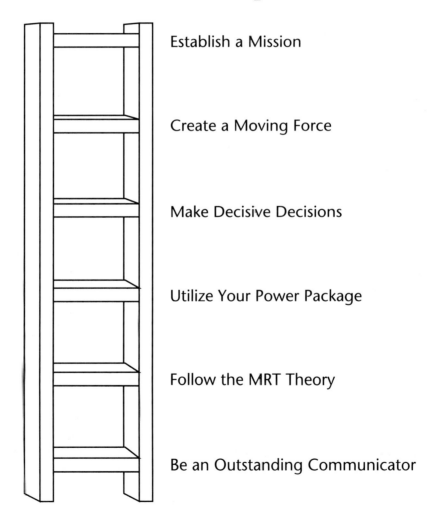

Establish a Mission

Create a Moving Force

Make Decisive Decisions

Utilize Your Power Package

Follow the MRT Theory

Be an Outstanding Communicator

Be an Outstanding Communicator

To be a good manager, it may be enough to be an average communicator. To be a good leader—and climb the first rung on the leadership ladder—you must do better. *What does outstanding mean?* It means that you:

▶ Convert your employees into followers, by keeping them informed to the point they know where you want to take your business

▶ Perfect your skills in directing a staff meeting

▶ Acknowledge that communication is the life-blood of any relationship

▶ Set up a two-way communications system within your business, so that communication flows up and down

▶ Are an outstanding listener

▶ Are willing to spend more time communicating, *and be better at it* than a good or excellent manager

▶ Will perfect your skills as a speaker in front of a group and as a small-group leader, and your counseling competencies or one-on-one communications

Communications is the glue that builds a team and holds it together. Employees will follow you only when they know what is going on.

EXAMPLE

Donna decided to establish a small deli specializing in Armenian food. During the first year, she did all of the ordering, cooking and managing herself. Things went so well that she soon hired a cook and three additional employees. Quickly, Donna found herself so occupied with management responsibilities—taking care of financial matters, ordering, spending time with customers—that she neglected communicating with employees. As a result Donna started to think of herself as a good manager, but not as a leader-manager. She was communicating, but she was not communicating enough. *The enthusiasm both she and her employees had the first year began to dwindle. Donna forgot to keep her team posted on how the operation was doing. She neglected to communicate her personal goals for the business. She spent too much time in her small office, working on figures and paper work, and not enough time outside leading the troops. Donna possessed the right instincts to be a good leader, but she allowed her management responsibilities to cover them up.*

It is hard for some small business operators to accept the fact that they must lead, as well as manage. And that leadership starts with a higher level of communication.

Follow the MRT Theory

As you will recall (see page 175) MRT stands for The Mutual Reward Theory. This theory states that to have strong and healthy relationships with others, both parties must eventually come out ahead. In other words, both parties must receive rewards and, as far as possible, the rewards should be equal. As a business owner, you stand to win big if your business succeeds. You will enhance your income, build an estate, have the ego satisfaction that goes with success, and so forth.

But what about your employees? Will you provide them with the rewards they need to stay enthusiastic and contribute at a high level to the team effort? What are the rewards you can provide them? If your business succeeds, you can provide some degree of job security, opportunities to learn and grow, job satisfaction, pride in being part of the team, and so forth.

Your employees will follow you—instead of just working for you—if they receive the right rewards. These are rewards that only you can give. It is true that good managers also provide rewards for those who work for them, but leaders provide enough rewards—and the right ones—that employees feel they are more a part of the team and share in the possibility of victory. Therefore, the turnover of personnel is higher under a good manager than a good leader-manager.

EXAMPLE

Ricardo is a quiet, hard-working individual who was a horticulture major in college. During his college years, he worked as a gardener for a small landscaping firm. Everyone accepted Ricardo as a good manager but few recognized him as an excellent leader. Later he bought out his boss and decided to expand the operation into a retail and wholesale nursery.

Ten years later, Ricardo now has over thirty employees on his payroll and his total operation does over four million in sales. While in college, he had learned and accepted the MRT idea. When he bought out his boss, he put the theory into daily practice. Not only did he provide his people with well paying jobs (slightly above the average) and good benefits, he went out of his way to see that each individual had learning opportunities and many psychological rewards. For example, every three months he gave a picnic at a local park for employees and their families. As most of his employees were Hispanic, Mexican food was featured and the event soon became a tradition. Other rewards were: flex-scheduling, a section where free flowers and plants were available for employees, and recruiting part-time help from employee's families.

Ricardo created a *family feeling* among his staff, because he provided rewards employees appreciated. They learned that they would be treated fairly and would share in the success of the operation.

Utilize Your Power Package

As the leader and owner of your own business, you have certain powers over those who work for you. The role of owner gives you power that you can exercise to achieve your goals. This is called *role power.* You also have power through your actions, the way you speak, and the manner in which you influence others. This is your *personality power.* On top of this, you have power because you know more about your business than anyone else. This is your *knowledge power.* The three sources of power together are your *power package.*

As the boss and leader, your role power should be assumed but not verbalized ("I'm the boss around here"). Do not let it go to your head to the point you are called the *dictator.* It is far better to be a quiet, sensitive, understanding *boss* than an overbearing one. Still, being the boss gives you power, and it is yours to be used appropriately.

Personality power should be used to influence employees to excel and reach goals. Sometimes it can be used in a staff meeting, sometimes during one-on-one counseling, and often *turned on* to influence customers and suppliers. *Your business should be, and is a reflection of your personality.* It is vital that you be true to your personality; be natural and what you really are. It is just as true that you should *use it*. In establishing a business of your own, your personality may be your primary source of power.

You should use your knowledge power primarily to teach your employees how to perform. Although you may be able to employ people who already possess knowledge necessary to your business, it is often best to start with employees who have the capacity to learn from you. When you act as a teacher and an employee learns her or his job from you, greater loyalty and productivity often result. You want to use your knowledge power to make the right decisions in finance, marketing and production, but its best use may be on the human side, where you train others.

EXAMPLE

Everyone knew that Mr. K was boss of the automobile service center chain; he was careful not to over-use it as a source of power. He would often put on a pair of overalls and pitch in to help change a set of tires or install a muffler. He did this so that he could use his knowledge power, so that his staff would respect him. But when it came to utilizing his personality power, Mr. K really turned it on. Not so much with employees, as with customers and resources. Everyone enjoyed his enthusiasm and sense of humor. People often remarked that he had built the chain with his outgoing and irresistible personality.

Make Decisive Decisions

It is said that managers make decisions, and leaders make decisive decisions. In fact, they often stage them so that they can demonstrate their leadership. Operating a small business requires that a stream of decisions be made every day. To be sure, many are minor decisions, like giving permission for an employee to leave work early to keep a dental appointment; others are major decisions that involve the direction the company will take. Whether a minor or major decision, once you have made up your mind, announce it with vigor and enthusiasm.

I once knew a master teacher who was so effective with students and so highly respected by colleagues that he was invited by the board of trustees to be president of the college. He lasted only one year. Why? He could not make decisions quickly and announce them in a decisive manner. In other words, he was an outstanding teacher, but a weak and ineffective leader.

When you make a major decision, it is always a good policy to consult with others, especially your own staff. But if you consult with others too long, the business suffers. Operating a business is a decision-making enterprise. Right or wrong, your staff wants you to make them without being wishy-washy.

Create a Moving Force

The next to the last rung on the leadership ladder is to be a dynamic force—a source of energy, enthusiasm and motivation for everyone around you. True leaders generate activity around themselves. They do this by giving out special assignments, holding staff members accountable, and generally stirring things up.

EXAMPLE

For the last three years, Dorothy has generated more sales as the owner of her own real estate office than any other agency in the country. With over twenty agents in the office, she creates an environment of activity that motivates others to the point they get twice as many listings and almost as many closings.

How does she do it? Is it because she is a wheeler and dealer herself? Is it because she is a mover and shaker? To some extent, yes. But equally important is the fact that she is always on the move. There is always a contest in progress to motivate her agents. She is active in her community, so that her agency has a strong image to attract both buyers and sellers. In essence, Dorothy seems to activate a centrifugal force that pulls agents and clients in her direction.

To be a moving force, one needs to inspire others. Rather than simply work for you, employees want to follow you. You set a fast, involving pace and they climb aboard the bandwagon. Put another way, you utilize your power package—especially your personality power—to energize others. Along with managing your business, you are *leading*.

Establish a Mission

The last rung in the ladder is to create and communicate that your organization has a purpose or mission. It has a goal to accomplish—often something beyond profit.

Louise is establishing a private career and counseling center in a major city in California. The center provides both materials and personal services for customers who are involved in finding and preparing for the right career, pre-retirement planning and personality enhancement.

What is her mission? Louise intends to experiment with her small operation for two or three years until she develops a model that can be franchised throughout the country. Her primary mission is to help others; her secondary mission is to create a successful and growing business. Louise admits it is her primary mission that motivates her the most.

One reason religious book and gift stores have been successful is that the owners have a primary mission to serve God. Their secondary purpose is to create a profit. Not all small business operations have such an obvious mission. Often, showing a profit and reaching a certain volume of business is the primary mission and all that is needed. For many, owning a small business is highly motivating, because it allows one to establish an estate to leave to other family members.

The point in having a mission is to provide a goal or direction for you and your business. Like an individual, a business often needs an overriding purpose to succeed.

Climbing the leadership ladder is the basic challenge that faces every small business owner. A business, like a search and rescue team, needs to be *led*. When you become a star communicator, adopt and practice MRT, utilize your personal power package, make decisive decisions, become a moving force, and give your business a mission, you are leading yourself, your employees and your business towards success.

Without your strong leadership, your business is like a ship without a rudder.

Your Turn　　*Answer the following:*

- ► Which of the leadership qualities discussed in this chapter do you accept?

- ► Which might you eliminate? What characteristics would you add?

Build a leadership ladder of your own. Start at the bottom of the ladder and, rung by rung, add a behavioral characteristic you will develop to strengthen your leadership ability and make your business a success. Add only those characteristics you are committed to incorporate into your behavior.

My Leadership Ladder

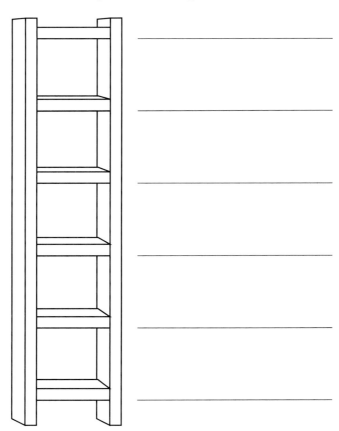

ASK YOURSELF

▶ Discuss your perceptions of yourself as a good manager and leader. Comment on the idea that being a good manager gives you the freedom to be a strong leader.

▶ How do you currently make the most of your power package? What do you intend to do to increase your personal power?

▶ Discuss the role and significance of establishing and articulating a clear mission for your business toward becoming a strong leader.

ABOUT THE AUTHOR

Elwood Chapman's self-help books have sold more than 2 million copies. He is well-known for his best-selling *Attitude, Your Most Priceless Possession, The New Supervisor, Comfort Zones,* and *Plan B: Converting Change Into Career Opportunity.*

A former professor of business at Claremont Graduate School, "Chap" as he is known to his friends, has spent many years as a business consultant. He recently retired and spends much of his time "on the beach" writing self-help books.

NOTES

NOTES

NOTES

NOTES

NOTES

NOTES

ABOUT CRISP PUBLICATIONS

We hope that you enjoyed this book. If so, we have good news for you. This title is only one in the library of Crisp's best-selling books. Each of our books is easy to use and is obtainable at a very reasonable price.

Books are available from your distributor. A free catalog is available upon request from Crisp Publications, Inc., 1200 Hamilton Court, Menlo Park, California 94025. Phone: (415) 323-6100; Fax: (415) 323-5800.

Books are organized by general subject area.

Computer Series

Beginning DOS for Nontechnical Business Users	212-7
Beginning Lotus 1-2-3 for Nontechnical Business Users	213-5
Beginning Excel for Nontechnical Business Users	215-1
DOS for WordPerfect Users	216-X
WordPerfect Styles Made Easy	217-8
WordPerfect Sorting Made Easy	218-6
Getting Creative with Newsletters in WordPerfect	219-4
Beginning WordPerfect 5.1 for Nontechnical Business Users	214-3

Management Training

Building a Total Quality Culture	176-7
Desktop Design	001-9
Ethics in Business	69-6
Formatting Letters and Memos	130-9
From Technician to Supervisor	194-5
Goals and Goal Setting	183-X
Increasing Employee Productivity	010-8
Introduction to Microcomputers	087-6
Leadership Skills for Women	62-9
Managing for Commitment	099-X
Managing Organizational Change	80-7
Motivating at Work	201-1
Quality at Work	72-6
Systematic Problem Solving and Decision Making	63-2
21st Century Leader	191-0

Personal Improvement

Business Etiquette and Professionalism   032-9
Managing Upward   131-7
Successful Self-Management   26-2
Americans With Disabilities Act   209-7
Guide to OSHA   180-5
Men and Women—Partners at Work   009-4

Communications

Better Business Writing   25-4
Technical Writing in the Corporate World   004-3
Writing Business Reports and Proposals   122-8

Small Business and Financial Planning

The Accounting Cycle   146-5
The Basics of Budgeting   134-1
Credits and Collections   080-9
Financial Analysis: The Next Step   132-5
Personal Financial Fitness   205-4
Starting Your New Business   144-9
Understanding Financial Statements   22-1
Writing and Implementing a Marketing Plan   083-3